Stephen Jenkinson

Money
and the Soul's
Desires

A Meditation

In memory of
Gwen Jenkinson 1927–2000
daughter of sorrows
making her way home

Contents

Acknowledgements

There is no such thing as "self-taught." Anyone describing themselves that way has a fool for a teacher. What your frailties and family and this world don't teach you, your friends and adversaries and the other world will. This book is a prayer shawl, a tool bag, and a bed blanket, woven from the earth-coloured threads offered by many cities, several countries, past ages, relatives uncounted and unknown, and characters of all kinds met on the road in and out of town.

My truest teacher and enduring spirit to the end of my days, master storyteller and defender of a world stitched together in ragged kinship, Brother Blue (Dr. Hugh Hill) of Cambridge, Massachusetts, taught me the flaming majesty and eloquence of the spoken word, and the triumph and fierce power of a rooted, initiated man who stands, courts danger, and loves life. Whatever good I've done with language since, I am hopelessly in debt to him. During our travels in the old days, he and his wife, oral historian Ruth Hill, opened their arms to this homeless and hurt-hearted white kid from another country and gave me a family when I had none. They claimed me as their own, and I miss them and honour them every day.

I also thank from my heart the two friends who were there from the first hatching of a boney, featherless, and teetering little dream that now lives as this book:

The American poet Thomas Smith crossed time zones and international borders in a bus in the middle of the night to stand with me, and his faithful, enduring friendship in the years before and since is my joy. He was the first to blow wind into the sail of my little writing boat and I remember him daily, and honour him and love him as my brother and my companion in defending life.

The Canadian broadcaster Tim Wilson sat staring off into nothing with me in a hard time with no reward or encouragement, and he was probably the first to wonder with me about money. His patient endurance kept the coals warm until I could make fire with them, and I touch my hat in gratitude.

I remember the faith and testimony of Michele Chaban, who has stood with me for a quarter-century in every self-induced, crazy weather, and who pointed these words in the direction of a book. Her heart is turned toward the holy, and she is kin to me.

ACKNOWLEDGEMENTS

I treasure the companionship and huge-heartedness of Alva Orlando, who tolerated the unrepentant self-absorption that seemed necessary at the time to hatch these embryo ideas into something that looked like life, and who loved me anyway.

Robert Bly and Martín Prechtel have been generous and brilliant teachers to me through their spoken and written words and I thank them for their tenacity and courage in chasing down dangerous ideas and feeding them to a crazed and ravenous and sorrowing culture. I remember their skill and cunning and tremendous love for life in what I do, and take heart from their presence in this world.

Christopher Lowry, bioregionalist and champion of hurt children in war-soaked lands, endured an early draft of this book and spilled his considerable, quiet, and humble brilliance over my revisions. My debt to him is paid a little in the offerings from him that are stitched into this homespun tapestry.

My old friend Buz Nickerson has tolerated years of my strangeness with his humour and open heart, and he gave me the basement room where the frayed threads of this little book were first braided together.

My friend and helper, pastor John Groen, kept me fed and clothed against the odds in the early days of this book, and I am always grateful to him.

I remember my two faithful friends and artists from the West, the wilderness defender and courageous, propulus-scented sentinel-maker Peter von Tiesenhausen, and the steady, colour-soaked sage gatherer Lorenzo Dupuis. Their beauty is in these pages, and both are fathers in spirit to many.

ACKNOWLEDGEMENTS

The nameless and almost structureless men's group in Toronto is an unruly nest of passionate, articulate, and soulful characters who are close to my heart. For some reason they took me in and continue to put up with me.

Gord and Beth McMillan and their big and generous family at Golden Lake have given me home shelter, stories, and a path into the Ottawa Valley bush, all of which feed me every day.

I remember Father Henri Nouwen, with whom I talked about money and soul. In gratitude, years later, I lift this book up to his spirit.

I thank editors Steven Beattie and Kathryn Dean for their honouring and patient tolerance of my beginner's blunders and ornery voice.

All teachers, friends and accomplices, fellow conspirators, lovers, and defenders of the sacred not named but treasured; their scent lifts off these pages, and I remember them.

My sister, Aprile Jenkinson, and her husband, Richard Alexandrovich, have made my best travels possible, and their generosity lives in these pages.

All my former in-laws and out-laws, whether they meant to or not, helped me see a world I knew nothing of, and I am grateful.

The noble and courage-filled people who have come to work with me, who have shouldered the tasks of soulful life in the face of ordinary and extraordinary hardship, hurt, heartbreak, and homelessness, and who have done me the great honour of allowing me to help them and to learn from them, are among

ACKNOWLEDGEMENTS

my greatest teachers.

My daughter, Jesse, queen of the house and faithful attendant in my lost years, has blessed me over and over with clear-eyed wisdom. She has remembered well in forgetful times and given me reason for pride and faith in the time coming after me.

My son, Gabriel, shows me the grace of his brawny warrior heart. I remember him taking his canoe out through the mist alone, and I honour him and kiss his brilliant feet for finding their own brilliant way.

I bless and honour the Great Mystery that has many times shown me death but held me from it, more than once fed me slowly back to health, planted my feet in this world, and kept my hunger for life keen. This book is a small offering in gratitude and faith of a promise made and kept.

Stephen Jenkinson
Toronto, Canada
February 2002

Introduction
A Brush With Big Money

Some years ago I travelled in Japan, and a business-man of my acquaintance there told me about an ingenious connivance he and his friends had come up with. The cost of living being what it was at that time, venerable men of moderate means had to choose a new restaurant with consid-erable care. He and his friends concocted a brilliant test. They would sit down, and after careful and animated study of the menu, weighing all the combinations of taste and extrava-gance, they would order tea and rice all round. They would wade into that frugal rumour of a meal as if it were a banquet, then step out into the street entirely satisfied, applauding one another's style and grace. Later, they'd compare notes, and vote as to whether the restaurant was promising enough to return. The principle they calculated by was a simple one: if the chef could make a meal of something as naked and unadorned as tea and rice, then that chef could be relied upon to make most things well. If not, then anything else coming from the kitchen didn't hold much promise. The unspoken faith buried inside this little ritual was even more beautiful and simple: with nothing to hide behind, the chef's soul was embodied in the tea and the rice. My businessman friend believed that when you ate from a person's kitchen, you were eating from their soul.

There is an economy of soul in this brilliant scheme, as well as a well-placed concern for the state of personal finances. We are saying a lot when we say "an economy of soul," and it will take us this whole book to begin doing justice to the idea. Our word *economy* comes from two Greek words which can be translated as "the laws of the house," or more informally as "the way this place works." Our common use of the word is poorer by a good margin, you'd probably agree, but I like to think of the soul as having an economy. The soul is a sort of crossroads or gathering place or house, where all the inner business of a person is considered and reconsidered, weighed and sorted, and finally acted upon, and it has its laws and its ways of doing things. My friend's restaurant ritual shows both a soul's concerns and a soul's way of doing things. It is a good example of a soulful approach to life.

I have worked for many years now as a sculptor and crafts-man. Like all artists I struggled — and still struggle — to learn how to make things well. But an artist sooner or later finds that learning all there is to know about the mechanics and the physics and the tools of the art does not make an artist. Taken alone, that training makes someone a technician. The art is only born when the maker's soul comes into view. The way, the form, the shape, and the style of the artist's inner life have to be incarnated, or embodied, when the raw material and the tools are taken into the hands. Put another way, the apprenticeship of the maker is an apprenticeship to the chosen art, to the teacher, to the soul of the materials, and to the maker's own soul. Responding to the demands the materials and tools make is a powerful way for the habits of the soul to become more evident and more present. The discipline required to become an artist involves a love of the teacher and the materials — a soulful knowledge — as well as a knowledge of one's soul. The one reveals the other.

I wonder if it is at all possible to be an artist, like that, in money. Why do people not find this same feel of calling or vocation or soul-stirring aroused and fed in their money lives? Is money so very different from clay or paint or wood — or tea and rice? Is it any less a "natural material"? If it is possible to be an artist in money, surely a knowledge of one's soul is mandatory preparation for such a pursuit. And just as surely, the ways of one's soul, when one works in money, would be similarly revealed. Money is in many ways as simple and as basic as tea and rice. But why is money so hard? And where does all the trouble with money come from?

This is, I believe, a faithful book about money and the soul.

It is not a how-to book, be assured. It is not a book about how to triumph, how to score, how to have more and feel good about it, or how to live with less and not feel deprived. It is not a map to the good life. Instead, it is a kind of modest chronicle of an apprenticeship to the hard teachings that money has to offer. It is a book that has its beginnings not in success but in failure, and not in artistry but in unknowing. And a faithful book should have an honest introduction.

• • •

Years ago I built a house for my family. That house was the tangible expression of all my convictions and certainties about married life and family life, about committed life and monied life. Building a house is very much like building a little universe. During the design stage, every unconsidered idea about what is necessary and what is good in domestic life is considered over and over again. Planning gives way, after many months, to building, and to the nightmare contingencies that come with it. The project happened largely with a significant and generous interest-free loan from my in-laws, who were dyed-in-the-wool businesspeople. I recall very clearly trying to do the best job possible to persuade them that I was being responsible with the loan. I was desperate to bring the job in on time and at the projected budget — and I pretty much did so. But the accomplishment didn't deliver what I'd hoped. It didn't really buy their respect, and it didn't really buy self-respect either. If you build a house, you design it and make the arrangements, show up every day, intervene and advocate where necessary (i.e., constantly), do some of the labour your-self, walk the site in the evening when most people are resting, sweat out the delays, die a little every time it rains, become demented as the February snows blow through window open-ings in the walls that should have been closed and boil down the hallways where the hardwood should be — if you do all of this, and yet you have not earned the money that pays for the house, whose house is it?

The whole business took me more than two years, from design to moving in. During that time I had no real employ-ment or income. Once I had taken over the general contracting chores, the house became my job. Even before it was finished, the house received a lot of attention. It won a significant national architectural award and was reviewed in local papers and glossy European architecture journals. It was, I would say now, a great achievement, though it blew a big hole in my working life and my professional development years. I am still proud of it and think of it, when I think of it, as my own. We lived in the house less than a year, if I remember rightly.

The house had to be sold as part of the dissolution of the marriage. I received an award for the house at a gala ceremony on the same day I had to list it for sale. I have a clear memory of shaking hands with high-level politicians and being photo-graphed with dignitaries and Mounties, and thinking at that moment that the whole event was a charade: it wasn't even my house anymore. I can recall vividly that during our last summer in the house, while going through that living death of waiting for the lawyers to finish their dissection of things, a couple of friends offered me their opinions on what went wrong, without my asking for them. Of all things, they suggested that I might think about how money had screwed things up.

Money had screwed things up. I was completely unprepared for that — so much so that I doubted it severely, took subtle offence at my friends' unsolicited advice, and didn't think about it much. Months later, while I was trying to re-establish the psychotherapy practice that I'd more or less abandoned to build the house, I had far too many hours of sitting in a borrowed office, staring and suffering, waiting for the very infrequent interviews with clients to come, wondering what to do, wondering whether anything would ever be all right again. Somewhere in there I recalled my friends' unwelcome observation, and it came to me one day, with nothing else to do, to write down all the stories I could recall where money had shown up somehow in the marriage. I didn't look only for stories where money had caused problems, but just for any recollection of where money was part of the story. I was surprised. There were a lot of stories in which money figured, many more than I'd thought there'd be. Writing them down took several days. And then I wondered what these stories had in common. And then — the hardest part — I tried to imagine what I'd been thinking at the time these events took place, or worse still, what I hadn't been thinking about. I was dismayed to find how difficult it was to remember honestly. I was more than dismayed to find how embarrassing, and how unsavoury, the whole business was, and the more stories that came, the more humbling it was. This book is built, stone by stone, from those painful and unpromising beginnings.

• • •

Here is the first story I wrote. I found it pretty unsettling at the time I remembered it, and I've still not entirely made my peace with it. Many years ago now, after I had been married a short while, my father-in-law sent me a message that he wanted to talk with me. It was an unusual request, since he rarely said anything to me and our conversations were always a bit awkward. I was usually a little uncomfortable in his home. He was a man of a certain swagger. He struck me as a man who was both self-made and self-enclosed. He was also chronically ill, so his bedroom was his office. To be called there was like being summoned for an audience with a potentate. For an outsider like myself, it was a kind of Oz. It was his boardroom, where all the worldly decisions were made. He was a wealthy man, and by all accounts he had been a genuine hustler in his earlier years. He'd scrambled up from very unpromising beginnings, and even with all his infirmities he hadn't surrendered any of the authority rich men have when they tell you what to do. What was negotiation in my world was edict in his. Through him I'd heard and seen more about money than I thought there was to know. He lived in a world that was just about totally unimaginable to me.

So, while the television nattered away in the corner, I sat, tried to make small talk — something I still haven't developed a knack for — and waited to find out what I was doing there.

He made small talk back, which was equally difficult for him. Presently and without prelude he cut to the matter on his mind. "Are you saving money?" he asked.

I heard the words clearly, but I really had no idea what he was asking. No idea at all. Now, I've had some work-related courtroom experience in the years since that day. I've learned that a good rule of thumb to remember while on the stand is: when asked a question, you are under no immediate obligation to answer that particular question, in those particular terms, at that particular moment. You can talk about something else and appear to answer the question, or you can direct the discussion elsewhere while you are sorting out your position on what you're being asked about or scrambling to respond. This requires a certain amount of maturity and poise and presence of mind, though, none of which are much available when you are young, newly married, and faced with a wealthy father-in-law. So, pretty much inevitably, and with a queasy foreboding, I caved in to the question.

"Yes, I'm saving a bit," I said.

That wasn't entirely true, mind you. I had recently graduated, and the job I'd found was much more for the experience than it was for the money. But that was the answer that came to me, to reassure him that I was trying to be responsible, that I was taking care of business, that his daughter and granddaughter weren't living in irredeemable hardship. I was trying to talk his language, see things his way, and live at that moment in his eyes, with no success at all.

Then he asked, "Are you doing without?"

Well, I thought, sure. Don't they go together? Isn't that what saving means, that you do without? It's a choice you make, it's an honourable one — and how else do people do it? Under his blank and unblinking gaze, I began to wonder, Where is this going? Now I was a bit unnerved, and suddenly I couldn't tell what was at stake, or what we were really doing in that conversation. There was a right answer, but I could see from his expression that it wasn't likely I was going to find it.

So, I nodded yes. Wrong answer. He pointed to the valuable things around the room and on the walls. Then he opened his arms in a grand and dramatic gesture as if to embrace the well-appointed house that lay outside the bedroom door, and he leaned toward me, and in a voice made of equal parts pity and dismay that he probably reserved for use on entry-level hirelings, my father-in-law said, "Don't do without. There's no need. Don't save."

That was an amazing moment in my life, looking back on it now. The prospect of not having to save — this had never occurred to me before. Saving was part of living as far as I'd ever thought about it. You work/you save/you work . . . There was no such thing as not saving — no such thing, that is, until that moment. This father-in-law, who in my mind ruled an empire of people and property and money, leaning over and whispering "Don't save" was more than I could manage or make sense of or take in.

Sitting in my basement office and thinking about that short and awkward conversation years later, it began to dawn on me that this little talk about money prompted a response in me that didn't really seem to be about money at all. Instead, I felt as though the curtain had been pulled aside a little bit and I had been given a glimpse of the Garden of Eden. I had grown up in a fatherless family of limited means, with my mother doing other people's sewing to stay afloat and us being cared for by the old neighbour lady, and there I was, suddenly in the land of unlimited possibility. All the shackles of necessity and limit and responsibility and forced moderation rattled and loosened and began to fall away. Somebody was whispering something about the Tree of the Knowledge of Good and Evil, something that I'd never known before, something that I didn't even suspect was there. I did continue to save a bit after that, when I could, but I'd had a brush with Big Money, and I was never quite the same. Suddenly, subtly and strangely, dreams and projects and adventures were possible, maybe even likely. When I began to ponder all this years later, I suspected that it was more valuable to know what this brush with money had done to me, and why I reacted as I did, than it was to know about how, say, the stock market works, or how my father-in-law made and kept *his* money.

• • •

Growing up in a house that had neither money nor spiritual inclination, it surprises me that I have come to write something that tries to bring them together. I've learned hard lessons about money and the soul's desires in the days since that audience with my father-in-law. When you are unconscious about things like money and the project of living a spiritual life, their

INTRODUCTION: A BRUSH WITH BIG MONEY

meeting in the midst of your own life is much more like a collision than an awakening. They bounce off each other like
scrambling atoms under an electron microscope, then hurtle
crazily off in all directions. They do spark a little energy when
they collide, but not enough to keep any project going for very
long. This is a kind of excitement that has no nourishment in it.
It is almost a certainty that at some time money will make problems in a person's effort to live a good and soulful life, and this
would be true even for those who do not see a soulful life
as necessary or possible. The consternation that ensues can be
nourishing, but only if some awareness is brought to bear. The
struggle must be a conscious one, and it will cost each person
their naïveté. Discipline, discernment, and a shoulder to the
work are rudimentary requirements.

It seems to me now that the coming together of money and
the soul in this life is inevitable and constant. This might even
be a God-given thing. Money has as much to say about the
soul as the soul does about money, and their sudden troubling
appearance together in a person's life is one sign of what I am
persuaded is the benevolence that lies at the heart of this
world: when in the presence of one, you *can* do something
with or about the other. One of the projects of adulthood in
this culture must be to recognize this kinship between money
and the soul's desires and to make some kind of peace
between them. This is an idea that I know goes against the
grain for most of us. What I will try to do in the pages that
follow is to sketch out what the undertaking of soulful and
conscious consideration of money might be like, and how

money might help make the soul's ways come a little more
into view.

• • •

This is a story about the valuable struggle to live a good,
authentic, and soulful life, which includes, even embraces, the
role that money has to play in it. I am aware, as you are, that
money and the work of one's soul seem very much at odds. If
ever there was a marriage made to confound its partners, it is
the uneasy, common-law union of money and the attempt to
live in a soulful way. For our times, and perhaps for all times,
theirs has been a loose, belligerent association, steeped in
necessity and plagued by bad faith. The puritanical among us
swear off one while embracing the other. We have ended up
with a culture where money people might deny any spiritual
inclination and spiritually-inclined people just as often secretly
disown money. There's scarcely a full lesson to learn from
either side. It's likely that most people feel neither well off
nor spiritually inclined. This kind of segregation, which seems
so natural and so obvious — and perhaps even necessary —
means no one any good.

The men of my generation are struggling in a hundred ways
to embrace the projects of mature masculinity. The work isn't
going smoothly from what I can see, and there are difficulties
in many relationships that come out of this struggle. The older
men I work with often have no stomach any longer for the
struggle to live a soulful life. They are men who count the days

to retirement so they can leave such struggles to others. And I see scores of younger men, men under forty, who are scared to death of marriage, money, and manhood, and with good reason. Many have never seen a strong living example of how these jobs get done, and many have no faith that the work is worth the effort, or even possible. I had them, and the women and children in their lives, in mind when I wrote this book. I want to say to them that it is worth the effort, and it is possible. But, more than that, it is necessary.

So this is not a book about making or investing money. It isn't a blueprint for some financial planning. It doesn't tell you how to do anything with your money, or where it should go. I myself am not very knowledgeable about the world of high finance. I've never had what I'd call a lot of money, and there have been times when I didn't have much at all. I get easily confused by high-end calculations, and I am as intimidated by investment as the next person. I confess that I use someone to prepare my income tax, since I get lost in the forms too easily — much more lost than when I studied Greek or Coptic. I try here only to wonder out loud about some very confounding business, just as I've done in my counselling work over the years. The knotted and heart-breaking dilemmas described in this book are things that people have wondered about with me over and over. They come up time after time. The soul's struggle with money is an enduring and trustworthy companion in life.

In this book we are walking together over common ground,

ground so common that we are unable at first to see it at all. Some time in our personal and ancestral past we grew accustomed to walking in silence, neither speaking to each other, nor seeing what was all around us, nor hearing what that common ground might be saying. Now we are walking together, hands in pockets, through the woods at dusk, and on the dusty path we have found a strange stone, and we are holding it up in the fading light to see if there is anything worth keeping. I want to say that there is.

The Darkness in Money

*Happiness is the deferred fulfilment of a prehistoric wish.
That is why wealth brings so little happiness; money is
not an infantile wish.*
— SIGMUND FREUD, 1898

A: A Short History

The Western world knows Freud as an adamantly
secular and psychological man. And this is a psychological
way of saying what most people instinctively know: money
and happiness are not kin. Our experience tells us more than:
Money can't buy me love. It goes much further than that.
Experience says: Money will mess with love, and with friendship. It will mess with any desire to do good and to be good.
Money can turn a good situation strange in a hurry. We don't
see food the same way, or clothing, or shelter, or any of the

other elementary presences in our lives — although sex is closer to money than it is to food in its power to change things. But money is trouble. Has been. Will be.

Freud wrote that real happiness comes from the satisfaction of needs and hopes and dreams that were born in infancy. Growing up, he says, doesn't seem to change that. If there is a value or worth in money, it is a value that has no attraction or purpose in infancy. And since what makes us deeply happy doesn't change, money doesn't bring happiness. But there is more to the story. Money is not neutral. It is not just that money brings us so little happiness. Money brings heartache, betrayal, arrogance, alienation, awkwardness, envy, suspicion, distortion, disgrace, and more.

Money fills us with a kind of fascinated dread. People will line up for hours to look at a display case with a million dollar bills in it, or a stack of gold bars. They will take pictures of the family gathered around this wonder. It's the closest they might ever get to a holy of holies. People in supermarkets will read stories of the rise and fall of millionaires or lottery winners with glee and envy, simply because they were millionaires. The noble sentiments and abilities of people often go missing when the golden calf is rolled out. There is both attraction and aversion when money is around. Why is *that*?

When I read Freud's easy dismissal of money, it made me wonder: Could there be any other reason why money doesn't bring happiness? Is it the *purpose* of money to bring happiness? Maybe the troubles with money don't come from the fact that it frustrates individual prehistoric wishes. Maybe those troubles don't come from human frailty. This chapter is going to explore the possibility that the turbulence money brings doesn't require a troubled *personal* history of money dealings at all. Instead, I'll try to show how money has a kind of mythic power that detonates subtle and subterranean things in people. In that sense our reactions to money are more than individual psychological reactions to individual psychological problems. Maybe the trouble with money is nothing personal.

"Nothing personal," though, is a hard idea to sell in Anglo North America, a place that believes so desperately in being self-made, self-taught, and self-enclosed, a place built by very efficient refugees, as healer and teacher Martín Prechtel calls us. Refugees tend to have a sense of personal identity that comes only from personal memory. Very little of that personal identity comes from inheritance or from the past. If someone asks, "Where do you come from?" we will likely name the last city or town we lived in, or the first. If someone asks, "Who are you?" we will tell the tale of what we have done, leavened maybe by tales of what has been done to us. In the West, the past seems to cast a short, faint shadow.

But there is another presence alongside the personal identity, a deeper identity that personal memory has a hard time acknowledging. It is a presence that has depth, subtlety, and valence. It includes bloodlines and ancestors, tribal allegiance and racial identity. Ultimately, it is a species memory that speaks through us. It endures in a person the way DNA endures, without intent or awareness. The Spanish poet Juan Ramon Jiminez sounds as though he's thinking psychologically about the personal unconscious when he writes:

> *I am not I.*
> *I am this one walking beside me*
> *whom I do not see.*
> *Whom at times I manage to visit,*
> *and whom at other times I forget;*
> *who remains calm and silent when I talk,*
> *and forgives, gently, when I hate,*
> *who walks where I am not,*
> *who will remain standing when I die.[1]*

But I hear the voice of this other presence, a presence that is not created by birth nor extinguished by death, a presence that is not owned or made individually, but is shared across boundaries of creed, history, and grievance. This is the "prehistoric" memory, which both informs and haunts the personal memory.

What does all this have to do with money? Money is a powerful and volatile influence in people's lives, in the same way that prehistoric memory is. Under its apparent commonness and familiarity, money comes to us arrayed in strange and ancient cloth. Money is a conjuring, mythological presence in the human world. Not only does money arouse prehistoric wishes — for safety, security, plenitude — that it cannot satisfy, but it also stirs a host of prehistoric and collective anxieties that it cannot soothe. It makes hungry where most it satisfies, to paraphrase Shakespeare. Its utter foreignness whispers something to us about individual, collective, ancestral, and species memories and histories and identities. Money is prehistoric in this way. This is the kind of idea that slips under the radar of the literal, rational, demythologizing mind, the kind of mind that dominates Western education, politics, public discourse, and, for the most part, spiritual and business practice. This is the kind of mind that most of us are heir to.

B: The Roots of Dread

*A man that is born falls into a dream like a man who falls
into the sea. If he tries to climb out into the air as
inexperienced people endeavour to do, he drowns.*
— JOSEPH CONRAD

Well, we're in it now. What is this thing, money? How did it
happen? What did people do before money was around?
Beneath the economic theories, the barter and monetary sys-
tems, the investment funds, the requests for spare change, and
the plans to retire at fifty, what is money, really?

Try to think about it not as something you either have or
don't have. Consider money for a moment as just an *idea*. The
first thing to notice is how many wild adjectives there are
around it. Money, in fact, is a kind of language, and people
who are good with language can help us to ponder the
questions we're asking. The American poet Wallace Stevens
wrote, with the right kind of delicate indecision, that "Money
is a kind of poetry." For most of his writing life Stevens was a
Connecticut insurance man, so he can be trusted to know
whereof he speaks on this point. And not only did he write
about money and work with it, he lived with it: his wife was
used as the model for the head on a version of the American
dime.

Charles Olson, Stevens' countryman and fellow poet, went
a bit farther, describing the cryptic nature of money in this
suitably cryptic way:

the under part is, though stemmed,
uncertain is,
as sex is,
as moneys are,
facts to be dealt with as the sea is . . .[2]

I'm going to use Olson's poem as a kind of overture to the themes of this chapter. Olson says, awkwardly, "moneys," as if there were more than one kind. And he says that when it comes to money, not all is there to be seen, for money has underparts to it. Money is "stemmed," tethered to the earth in some way and not hovering. This means that money has roots which show, a history and a story which can be read and known and learned from if it can be endured. He says that moneys give us facts "to be dealt with as the sea is," which has some ominous overtones when you consider that there are no deals to be made with the facts of the sea.

The facts of money, though, are not immutable, and so are not really facts as we normally use the term at all. The facts of money more resemble the facts of sex — volatile, unbridled, a bit menacing at times, and ultimately more strange than attractive. That is a fulsome thought, when you ponder the volatility of the "facts" of sex, and when you ponder the lengths to which we go to keep sex and money apart in civilized company — something we will look at in Chapter 5. And these facts resemble the sea more than anything else. Both the sea and money change their faces in an instant, without notice, consideration, or malice. Olson's little stanza has a "Render unto Caesar" ring to it: you feel as though you are being told something that you might need to know, but you don't know exactly what that is, or what to do about it.

● ● ●

I've already tipped my hand, as you've seen. The power of money doesn't come primarily from the way it buys things or allows people to control other people. Money's power comes from its mystery and its primitiveness. When we're tracking something as wild and elusive as money, we need to think as money thinks, see as money sees, be as money is. Metaphor and myth are going to be more valuable to us than economics or psychology, which is why I rely on the poets here, and not the economists.

What does it mean to say that "Money is as the sea is?" How are the two alike? Try to remember what your primary school science teacher said about the physics of water. First, it is water's nature to have no nature of its own. It is an exquisite and irreducible mystery. Colourless and odourless when left alone, water has no shape, and probably no movement. Instead, it is very impressionable, and it absorbs almost anything that presses upon it. Water is spineless and boneless, and only the water spider can find its skin, it seems. It takes the shape of any container. Once fouled, it is fouled entirely and has no vestige of purity. It has no stable state, going from solid to liquid to gas with minimal influence or encouragement. It generally comes in volumes of "too much" or "not enough," depending on whose irrigation needs are being met. Though not strong at all, enough water can carry any weight to any destination for eternity. It has no mood of its own, no tone, no feeling. In a phrase, it has no inherency. Though ubiquitous, it does not endure. Standing by itself, water means nothing. Its meaning, its purpose, its function, and its value — they all come from elsewhere. It is a kind of void: full of associations, empty of content. That is its essence.

The sea shares many of these same characteristics, but its sheer magnitude multiplies them exponentially. It is changeable to the point of being fickle, indifferent to the point of malevolence. It is unmanageable, uncontrollable, unpredictable. To be "at sea" in one's life is not a good thing. There is no "place" in the sea, and no place to be. Despite our best navigational technology, and despite being helped by the stars and by satellites, our instincts say that when on the sea there is only an approximate "here" or "there." At best, mankind has an unequal, jittery, dependent partnership with it. Its surface is a kind of betrayal, because it promises so much and conceals so much. The sea is a fact, of course, but it is also a myth.

The early twentieth-century Spanish poet Antonio Machado, a landlubber all his life (most of it spent teaching school in a small town in a semi-arid region of southern Spain), offered this strange and somewhat grim advice to those who are at sea, both literally and figuratively:

Mankind owns four things
that are no good at sea;
Rudder, anchor, oars
And the fear of going down.[3]

This little poem has fierceness and fascination in it, and a dead reckoning about where the source of things is. Using your ear attuned to the unspoken, you can clearly hear Machado saying, "Go down." All the things that keep you afloat may keep you dry — but they will also feed your dread. They most certainly will keep you away from the abyss, and so from the things that need knowing. Staying dry and staying clean keeps the dread whole, intact, and unfamiliar.

The Creation story in Genesis is one of the foundation myths of the Judeo-Christian tradition. It is an account of the beginning of the natural order, but it is also a catalogue and a map of human fears about our place — or lack of it — in the world. Throughout this account there is an air of menace and alienation. God hovers over the waste and emptiness of the primeval deep, and only after some order is wrestled from the chaos is any of Creation called "good." Humanity has no hand in creating the world. Instead, we are invited to "rule . . . over everything," dominating, domesticating, and defending ourselves against all living things. The story of Creation begins in anarchy and ends in an uneasy remoteness from the natural world, and soon enough from each other. Genesis helps us to recognize just how deep and enduring this dread of Creation is.

THE DARKNESS IN MONEY

Anyone who has been in peril far out at sea in a forty-foot
swell in a slowly sinking ship without a view of land and without the prospect of help, as I once was, knows these things in
their bones. They also know this culture's deep fear that the
fathomless depths are not really plotting our destruction, as the
uninitiated among us would imagine. In a desolate age like our
own, hostile to myth, the deep is instead merely indifferent.
Nature, biologist Stephen Jay Gould wrote, is as she is: amoral
and persistent. She doesn't give a damn for humans, nor does
she recognize the precious entitlement to life people believe
in. For humankind, that indifference is worse, because lonely
people sense menace in remoteness. This kind of experience
is as close as many might come in this life to the sense of
cosmic indifference that the Creation myth places at the very
origin of the world. That is the place where this mediaeval
French prayer comes from:

Lord, Help me . . .
Because my boat is so small,
and your sea so immense.

There is dread buried in this prayer. This anarchy, this dread
and alienation and darkened mystery, this prehistoric, mythic
memory of being homeless in a menacing world, all embodied
in the sea, is all dredged up by money. Money has some
kinship with the mythic power of the sea, and the aversion to
money in our lives, the anxieties money causes us, is testament
to that fact. Our feelings about money are not idiosyncratic,

quirky, or transitory. They are primitive, with a well established history and lineage that extends far beneath personal experience. Money, it seems, does resemble the sea.

While most of the adjectives that gather around money more accurately describe our *relationship to money*, or our feelings about it, a few are closer to describing its own essence, its nature. Chief among these is the character of liquidity. Money runs to and fro, it ebbs and flows, it can be frozen, it floats, rises, and falls. It buoys up, it evaporates. It floods. You could be drowning in it, or you could be left high and dry by it, or you could be carried away by it. It is nothing. It is everything. It is only money.

The liquidity of money is perhaps the thing that we find to be its least trustworthy aspect, the queen of our misgivings. Money has no meaning of its own. To illustrate this I've often held out a five-dollar bill to my clients and asked, "What does this mean?" I've usually had befuddlement for an answer, because people are so unaccustomed to thinking this way about money. People are much more attuned to what money "can do" for them, or to them, than to what money is, or to how it does what it does. Try this on yourself, and listen carefully to what comes up. You are likely to find that much of the bill's meaning will flow from ancillary questions. Answers may come only if you ask, for instance: "Well, who's holding the money?" That qualification can change relationships between people in an instant, and it shuffles all aspects of the meaning of money.

So it might be clear now how money has a certain physics

to it. Chief among those qualities are fathomless fluidity and volatility. But money is also transparent, and can become anything we want it to be. Jorge Luis Borges, the South American writer, puts it this way in a short story called "The Zahir":

> In Belgrano Street I took a cab. Sleepless, obsessed, almost happy, I reflected that there is nothing less material than money, since any coin whatsoever ... is, strictly speaking, a repertory of possible futures. Money is abstract, I repeated; money is the future tense. It can be an evening in the suburbs, or music by Brahms, it can be maps, or chess, or coffee; it can be the words of Epictetus teaching us to despise gold.[4]

It can also become what we don't want it to be. It rarely endures, yet as a worry or a burden, it is always around. Like water, its memory, purpose, and function come from Somewhere Else.

Why is money trouble? A better question to ask is: What happens to us when we are in its presence? Money creates so very little in a person, and intensifies so very much. Just as water adds volume and little else, money reveals and magnifies what was there beforehand. Perhaps it is truer to say that, just like water to light, money distorts that which passes through it. For this reason money seems like a seducer and a betrayer, as something having such a calm surface and such mysterious and harsh submarine machinations. It is something whose neutrality is itself a guise, like a calm sea. Of themselves, though, money and water create nothing. In this way both may be thought of as quite pure. Imagine money being pure! Like water, money has a hundred functions and no character.

I do some work for the Palliative Care unit of a general hospital. Death is either coming or going all the time. I see many people come to this confrontation waiting for the Big Realization, the moment when all is revealed, when wisdom is won, when charity and brotherhood and forgiveness are achieved. And it almost never happens. What happens instead is that people die as they have lived, for the most part. The approach of death does not make a new person, nor does it create a spiritual genius. It intensifies the person who is already there, sometimes to an intolerable degree. At the approach of death, people often become a more adamant version of who they've been all along. Death, in this way, is a lot like money.

● ● ●

There is an old world-weariness that says, with resignation and dread, that money is the root of all evil. This aphorism seems to have circulated with as much liquid acceptance and conse-quence in the West as money itself does. It is used as a time-tested warning, and it sounds as if it has biblical author-ity. It has that end-of-the-world self-evidence about it, as if only someone blind or evil would argue. It is also a rather telling misquote of a biblical passage, I Timothy 6:10. Like all misquotes, especially ones that reappear as if newly minted for each generation, it is much more telling than any faithful remembering of the text could be. It is telling in the way that Freudian slips are telling.

The letter to Timothy actually says, "For the love of money is the root of all evil." What is to be made of the common omission of "the love of . . ."? I am making the case here that money does confound people, and it can be particularly confounding to those who are spiritually inclined. Leaving out the reference to the love of money probably indicates a desire for a gross simplification of a very subtle truth. If you think that it is necessary to curse money in order to live a spiritually intact life, then you have a simple remedy for the imprecisions and anxiety that money arouses in you. Once money is evil, the avoidance of money, or the cursing of money, is the key to blessedness. Just don't get attached to it, and you'll be all right. If, on the other hand, you are obliged to question your attachments and your loving as the passage from I Timothy implores you to do, you are back inside the convolutions of your spirit's work. You are courting the questions again. These kinds of levelling, simplifying, and literalizing instincts, and the ambivalence they hide, abound around money. This, after all, is our theme: money itself provides the occasion for finding this kind of deep ambivalence in the self, and money is one place where the soul's work must be done. That is the real invitation extended by the biblical passage. That is the real salvation buried in the verse.

So it is not a bad thing that this misquote persists, because it allows the levelling and simplifying instincts that seem to gather around thorny life problems like money to be met and recognized and understood. There is a mania for resolution in this culture, a sad insistence that differences should cease being different, that certainty and sameness should prevail, that mystery should surrender, that the stranger should stop being strange. The rationalist solution for mystery is consumption. The rational way of "understanding" is to eliminate the unknown. If a Westerner wants to understand another culture or spiritual tradition, he buys it. The Greek verb which is the root of our word "mystery" means, "to close the mouth," suggesting that silence, not consumption, is called for when mystery is present. The Dagara culture in Burkina Faso, West Africa, unrelated to Greece or Anglo-America, offers the same warning. Malidoma Somé says that his language has no specific word for the supernatural. "The closest we come to this concept is *Yielbongura*, "the thing that knowledge can't eat."[5] Conspicuous consumption of the mysteries and the vagaries of life is a Western way of knowing, but precious little survives that kind of hunger.

So we need some other kind of approach for this inquiry, one that is in deeper sympathy with the mythic dimensions of life that exist beneath the radar of the rationalist mind. In the rest of this book, we'll resist the temptation to swallow the mystery we're trying to understand. Instead, we'll try — in small doses, at least — to be swallowed by it.

• • •

Like Nature itself, human nature seems to be terrorized by a vacuum, and rushes to fill it somehow. If we could call the gap between real monetary value and the symbolic value in money a vacuum, we could see how the old practice of placing a face on coin and paper currency is a conscious, ritualized impulse to fill it. This is what "face value" is supposed to do: calm money down, put a halter in its mouth, and make it serve. The demonization of money, the fear of money, the proscriptions against money all testify to the old mistrust of anything feral and unbroken. If it is true that money doesn't have a face of its own, then it is certain that money securely and faithfully embraces the many faces we project onto it.

Money is by another name filthy lucre — that is the easy aversion many surrender themselves to — but it is *mysterious* filthy lucre. The taboos surrounding money in the rationalist West are, ironically, taboos about ritual defilement, about cleanliness and debasement. Adjectives of cleanliness and dirt are common in references to money. Sociologists and anthropologists give accounts of elaborate rituals for redemption from defilement in Aboriginal cultures. We in the West consider this an arcane novelty only because we are unconscious of our own similar impulses. But I recall the subtle signs of this conviction in my own house growing up. You washed your hands after handling money, or at the very least you avoided putting them near your mouth. The wooden cutting board in the kitchen, *guaranteed* to be infinitely more germ-laden, aroused no such alarm. Recently I saw a couple who were probably at the end of their marriage, and there was a lot of sadness in the room. At the end of the session, when it was time to pay, the man pleaded advanced age and embarrassedly admitted that he had forgotten his chequebook. "I'll come by later," he said, "and clean it up."

The impurity of the material world, a feeling that money so easily denotes, mirrors a prejudice we have about the impurity of the body. What are we saying when we say we are "cleaned out"? Well, we've either used a purgative, or we are penniless. There are, no doubt, religious fanatics who may take pride in practising both, even at the same time, to achieve a kind of radical purity. Freud made great use of the common associations of money and fecal matter:

> The connections between the complexes of interest in money and of defaecation, which seem so dissimilar, appear to be the most extensive of all.
>
> In reality, wherever archaic modes of thought have predominated or persist — in ancient civilisations, in myths, fairy tales and superstitions, in unconscious thinking, in dreams and in neuroses — money is brought into the most intimate relationship with dirt. We know that the gold which the devil gives his paramours turns into excrement after his departure, and the devil is certainly nothing else than the personification of the repressed unconscious instinctual life . . . Indeed, even according to ancient Babylonian doctrine gold is the "faeces of Hell" (Mammon = *ilu manman*). Thus in following the usage of language, neurosis . . . is taking words in their original, significant sense, and where it appears to be using a word figuratively it is usually simply restoring its old meaning.
>
> The original erotic interest in defaecation is, as we know, destined to be extinguished in later years. In those years, the

interest in money makes its appearance as a new interest which has been absent in childhood.[6]

Freud is struggling with this. He was a man of his time, and the moral overlay in his comments is clear: there is something disgusting and base about a fascination with money. Yet he is trying to be scientific, and he knows he's on to something again. The denigration of money is not really a moral indignity, though there are all kinds of moral outbursts around it. Instead, it is a primitive loathing; this is the contention here. Though he seems to be diminishing their sophistication and their trust-worthiness, Freud is saying that there is this other kind of knowing available in myth, fairy tale, and the like. "Instinctual," "superstitious," "unconscious," and "archaic," fairly deprecating terms when levelled from a perspective like psychology, all describe this non-rational, non-literal other way of seeing that money seems to provoke. Freud knew money was strong med-icine, just as his patients did, but the demythologizing civility of the time seems to have robbed him of the opportunity to see all that was revealed by its uses and abuses. I think he came closer to the bone when he wrote that money brings little happiness because it doesn't answer the child's needs. The fascination that children have with shit, though, has its counterpart in adults' fascination with money. Fascination, exploration, and the rest, yes. But not happiness.

• • •

Finally, a note of caution. Psychology makes a lot of claims about things it believes are true and constant in the human psyche, regardless of tribe or time. These theories are often inflicted on non-Western or Indigenous people. It is possible, and likely, that Indigenous cultures past and present may not be troubled by money in the same way, and may not share the difficulties and dreads I've described, in part because their ancestral roots and memories grew elsewhere. As well, there are some Indigenous cultures that were colonized by European conquerors, and were obliged to surrender their own stories for myths like The Garden and The Fall, Heaven and Hell and the One True Religion; they may carry in some degree the prejudices I'm talking about.

There are non-Western cultures among us which share the traditional teaching that humankind has an uneasy and inconstant home in the world. But their response often tends to map out a program of reconciliation with Creation, rather than a domination. The relationship between humans and Creation that their myths embody is not one of indifference or ongoing warfare, but one of mutual dependence, one in which the natural order needs people and seeks out meaningful contact with us to sustain and nourish human life and the life of the world. The possibility of that kind of reconciliation has not survived most interpretations of the Creation myth, perhaps because it did not survive the myth itself.

Usury, the Shadow of Money

*A certain lawyer stood up
and put him to the test, saying,
"Teacher, what shall I do to inherit
eternal life?"*

And he said to him, "What is written . . . ?"

*And he answered, "You shall love . . .
your neighbour as yourself."*

*And he said to him, "You have answered correctly;
do this and you will live."*

*But . . . he said to Jesus, "And who
is my neighbour?"*
— LUKE 10:25–29

I remember being in an introductory political science class one fall morning in the early 1970s. We were in a giant lecture hall, which was still a novel thing in those days. The lecturer used a microphone, and he had a good sense of the theatrical for a poli sci man. I remember him dropping his voice to a whisper and saying, "There's only so much money in the world. (Long pause.) Only so much to go around. (Longer pause.) If you have some, chances are someone else doesn't." (Longest pause possible.) "Chances are," he said, "you have somebody else's. Chances are, you took it from them."

The majority of us in the lecture hall that day were fairly privileged people. Someone else was working at that very moment to pay our tuition, so most of us could be there, fixed upon our studies and undisturbed by the brute necessity of having to earn enough money to continue. Being protected and at least a little naïve, we were vulnerable to the challenges and attacks that disaffected academics sometimes launch upon untested undergraduates. We were targets. The offhand statements of the lecturer got to me. He didn't say these things harshly, as if to humiliate someone who hadn't reached the same conclusion. I suspect now that he wasn't blaming us, which would have been easy enough to do. But I was dazed by this very sudden and very unthought-of thought. Remembering it now, I can see that I had never really thought about money until that moment — at least, I'd never thought about how money felt to me. I'd never been conscious in the presence of money. This is like the kind of unconsciousness that you often have in the presence of the newly beloved: bewildered, strangely compelled, and your life is utterly changed. At nineteen, hearing this news and feeling this turmoil for the first time, I was rattled. I remember thinking, What have I been doing all this time, that I haven't thought of this? Where have

36

I been? I remember feeling that things had been happening all around me, big things, that I'd never been aware of. If you've ever had that twin feeling of astonishment and betrayal at finding that your life has been made all around you without your knowing about it, you will recognize this kind of moment. I was connected to all kinds of people through money. The sheer fact that this connection existed had some consequence that I neither intended, nor suspected, nor condoned: money made relationships, like an ambivalent, disguised Cupid — like a kind of angel.

In a culture that believes emphatically in self-determination and in the individualization of the psyche and the soul, as Anglo North American culture does, the idea that relationships are forged between us and others without our awareness or consent typically strikes us as unfair, unlikely, or unimportant. Despite the small dent made in my isolated certainty about the world that morning, it took me another fifteen years to recognize that the teacher was whispering something that was inevitable and necessary, something I needed to know to be a human being in this world.

This is a chapter about the history of usury. Woven into this ragged tapestry are lost lessons about brotherhood and kinship, and teachings about the explicit dangers to the soul, the neighbour, and the stranger of a culture-wide refusal to take these lessons and teachings to heart. As we shall see, the history of usury is also the story of a strange amnesia that has taken away our memories and our understanding of the practice, and how it has so often and for so long been used as a blunt-edged tool to keep the stranger strange. There is some grim material to be found in the interplay of money and the spiritual life through the last millennium of Western culture, and this should not be forgotten in a meditation like this one. Lessons heard but not yet lived through are easy to forget. So the best lessons are those that teach us how to remember and warn us about the perils of forgetfulness. It is worth knowing, for instance, that in the myths of classical Greece, the river that ran through the Underworld was called Λετηε (*Lethe*). The waters of that river were lethal to humans not because they could kill, but because they could induce crippling, blinding amnesia, which was many times worse. Those waters of forgetfulness are present in the Greek word for truth, αλετηια (*alethia*), which could just as well be translated as not-forgetting. Truth and fidelity, it counsels, are to be preserved by the cultivation of memory. The English language holds this notion, too. A more faithful opposite of the word *remember* could be *dismember*, the tearing apart of things that were once bound together. Remembering is restoring that original wholeness associated with truth and fidelity. Memory, truth, the ability to be faithful and act in an authentic way — all of these are bound together and depend on each other. And the Latin word *moneta,* from which comes the word *money,* is also the Latin name for the Greek mother of the Muses, Μνεμοσψνε (*Mnemosyne*) — the goddess of memory. Etymologically, money and memory are kin.

• • •

In a very fine book called *The Gift*, Lewis Hyde, the American poet and teacher, sets himself the task of sorting out different kinds of indebtedness. Hyde wonders what really distinguishes *gift* from *loan*. He shows that emotional and spiritual and social debts accrue to both, but that they are at root utterly distinct transactions, with different kinds of spirit attached to them, and they create, describe, and maintain different kinds of relationships. Usury, it seems, is a particular hybrid of gift and loan. It helps, but at a cost. Money loaned leaves the giver, but it comes back, the principal enhanced by the interest. Usury also secularizes money, by introducing the idea that this kind of transaction is free of spiritual consequence. Hyde wonders whether usury marks the transition from gift culture to market society:

> The idea of *usury* . . . *appears when spiritual, moral, and economic life begin to be separated from one another*, probably at the time when foreign trade, exchange with strangers, begins. When foreign trade begins, the tendency is to differentiate the material increase from the social and spiritual increase, and a commercial language appears to articulate the difference. In a gift society, the increase follows the gift and is itself given away, while in a market society the increase (profit, rent, interest) returns to its "owner" [italics mine].[1]

The language of commerce which we use today remembers this old division between spirit and money by hinting at this even older kinship between them. In a bank you can reconcile an account, redeem a coupon, purchase a bond, enter into a covenant, forgive a debt, and be forgiven one (though this last transaction is rare), or you may be given or extend a period of grace, also rare.

So money and the language of institutional religion go back a long way. You might think it would be natural and obvious that all religious traditions would cast aspersions on money or condemn it outright. While Judaism, Islam, and Christianity struggle with the subtle dilemmas that money poses for a community's spiritual practice, they do make room for money. In the end, these struggles are an attempt to establish what is permissible, or bearable, when the soul and money touch. What they say is: *there are different kinds of money.* For example, there is a verse in the Koran that neatly separates out which financial transactions are foreign to the religious spirit.

What ye put out at usury to increase it with
the substance of others, shall have no
increase from God.
— SURA 30:38.

Profiting in a spiritual way, through spiritual work, is a blessing, but should you want to profit materially through usury, you're on your own. God will add nothing to the gains of a usurer. Usury is a problem, the Koran says, because it moves the usurer away from God. It is almost as if the practice insulates a person from the presence of the divine. It is an interesting if not unexpected piece of advice, and it seems to reinforce the old fears that money and faith don't mix, and that God will abandon and forsake any place where usury is tolerated.

There is also a verse in the one of the five books of Moses which argues against the lending of money or goods for personal profit. However, in this case there is a condition attached.

> *You shall not charge interest to your countrymen: interest on money, food, or anything that may be loaned at interest.*
>
> *You may charge interest to a foreigner, but to your country-man you shall not charge interest so that the Lord your God may bless you . . .*
>
> — DEUTERONOMY 23:19–20

This rule appears in a long list of prescriptions and pro-scriptions which come from the struggle to define who is a Jew and who is not, who is kin and who is not. As the Jewish people had experienced an extended period of colonization, enslavement, and intermarriage, the preservation of kinship was a crucial part of recovering tribal identity. So the book of Deuteronomy attempts to establish some basic understanding of what constitutes normative Judaism in the wake of those experiences.

Like the Koran, the Mosaic law included injunctions against usury, but here there are gradations. Here there is subtlety. You can profit from usury, the law counsels, but not inside the tribe. Clearly, this is a prohibition based on the calculation: Who is my kinsman? And just as clearly, the suggestion is that usury, in this first era of the practice in the Judaeo-Christian tradition, is to be employed as a demarcation of kinship. It is a tolerable practice only beyond that circle of inclusion, only among strangers. This is surely not the only reading of Deuteronomy 23:19–20, but perhaps it warrants being pursued a little.

Why would usury between members of a clan or tribe be a problem? Well, usury is a very tricky proposition. Money loaned at interest to needy borrowers looks like a kind of qualified manna from heaven. It appears to help keep them afloat, probably when they need it most and are without any other recourse. At a broader level the lending of money at interest looks as though it keeps the world turning and the money flowing. Alas, not so. Usury ultimately arrests the circulation of money and goods. It retrieves them from the community and concentrates them around the lender. If money lent out in usury was a toy, it would be a yo-yo, not a ball. Usury in the end cuts the community off from the benefits of that money and those goods — and so cuts the usurer off from the blessings of the Lord. Usury is trouble, inevitably, in a homogeneous culture, because the spirit of usury (self-interest) is contrary to the spirit of community (mutual obligation). So says the law of Moses. And because the practice of usury itself is hostile to the spirit of brotherhood and to the workings of community, it is banished outside the city walls.

This banishment occurs in financial, political, and psychological ways. When money entanglements such as these are sent away, though, they don't disappear. They move just out of range of the normal light of inquiry and wonder, just beyond the frontier of concern. When that happens, money functions like a steady and scowling border guard, keeping the little self safe and the strangers out on the edge of town. The authors of Deuteronomy used the usurer to help maintain the boundary separating the neighbour from the stranger.

• • •

The contentious history of usury tells the sad story of the corruption of the ideal of brotherhood. This use of the practice to discern and mark fraternity appears to have worked as long as brotherhood was tribal, and the foreigner was outside the gate. The segregation was clear, and usury simply marked it. Later, it appears that Jesus took on the tradition of usury pretty directly. He did not just condemn usury or usurers outright. Instead, he challenged the old rationale for usury by insisting on a revolutionary reassessment of the nature of brotherhood, or kinship. His pronouncements on relations between strangers seem bent on lifting kinship away from race, culture, or even familiarity. When Jesus described the criteria for citizenship in the Kingdom of God, he moved brotherhood in a global or cosmic direction. Brotherhood after him could also be understood as a function not of blood or race, but of compassion or grace. Jesus raised the possibility that brotherhood functions by inclusion, not by exclusion.

Reshuffling the deck on tribalism and kinship brought tremendous anarchy to a culture accustomed to making money bear the burden of guarding the gate and keeping the stranger at a safe distance. That old and simple function of usury in marking the stranger became unworkable if any stranger was a potential brother. So many of Jesus' pronouncements and actions concerning money have this confrontational quality about them: the "render unto Caesar" riddle, the attack on the financiers and merchants in the temple, the forgiveness of debts advocated in the Lord's Prayer. His blurring of the boundaries of brotherhood was provocative to the quick. And this brings forward a hard question for a culture bent on imitating Jesus: if everyone is my brother and there are no more foreigners, where does money properly belong in my relations, and upon whom can I practise usury?

Early Christianity struggled with these irreconcilable threads in its own holy book. This is the second era of usury in that tradition. As is so often the case, in text and in life, the tension was resolved in a way that hid the tension. Fellow Christians now considered themselves brothers, whether related by blood or clan or nation. Former tribal enemies were brothers. All those who called themselves Christians were included in the economy of grace, and with them no usury was permitted. The Other, by contrast, was an unbeliever. All people had been given the opportunity to join the fellowship, but some separated themselves from God's grace by resisting conversion. Through obstinacy and arrogance they had deprived themselves of redemption and salvation, and lost Eden again. With them, as things developed, anything was allowed. That was the resolution that emerged. In the matter of brotherhood, Eden's gate was found at the usurer's scale. A fourth-century church father named St. Ambrose of Milan summed up this troubled resolution nicely:

> Upon him whom you rightly desire to harm, against whom weapons are lawfully carried, upon him usury is legally imposed . . . He fights without a weapon who demands usury; without a sword he revenges himself upon an enemy, who is an interest collector from his foe. Where there is the right of war, there is also the right of usury.[2]

Wars, bear in mind, were and are exercises in the assignation of brotherhood, just as surely as they were and are commercial enterprises. Though the benchmark for brotherhood may have changed as Christendom grew along the dying roots of the Roman Empire, the use of usury as a weapon for establishing and enforcing the distinction between friend and foe was not altered much. The result was an unconscious blurring of distinctions that confounded Western culture down to the Reformation. The stranger was no longer just a stranger. Because the stranger had resisted brotherhood, he had also become an enemy of the faith. Hyde puts it this way: "It does not seem to have occurred to [the Church Fathers] that the stranger could be someone who is not in the group and yet also not an enemy. As soon as all men *ought* to be brothers, all aliens become enemies."[3] The path was now made smooth for the Crusades and the Inquisitions. Money was being used to keep the stranger at a distance, and then to punish him for his strangeness.

The Church Fathers struggled to reconcile Christian law with Mosaic law. They did so using two fateful and tormented pieces of logic. In the first, the Church Fathers were obliged to accept the defence of usury in Deuteronomy because the Old Testament was God's word. So they determined that usury was a punishment inflicted by God upon both Jew and Gentile in that period. In the second, they subsumed Mosaic law under Roman or civil law: Christian law for the spiritual guidance of the Saved, Roman law for the daily governance of the Fallen. And usury was prescribed in Mosaic law. In Christian Europe, that same law was used to isolate or ghettoize those Jews who resisted conversion. Without having faced squarely the conundrum that Jesus brought to light through his strange answers to the question "Who is my neighbour?" the ecclesia took the usury dilemma one step further. There were two problems: usury, and those who resisted conversion. They were unresolvable irritants inside the body politic. Why not join them together? Why not make the stranger the usurer?

You know who got the job. Pagans got the job — mainly Jews. Since they were not going to be brothers anyway, why not let them do the dirty work? The word *pagani* at one time meant roughly "the uncultivated, uncultivating ones, those living outside the city walls" or beyond the fenced-off farms, out in the bush. There's a condemnation and a fear buried in the earliest meanings of the word, a condemnation of those who have not been domesticated and a fear of wild places and those who dwell there. Pagans were those who were outside the orbit of the urban centre, beyond the reach of the arbiters of orthodoxy. That is what made them barbaric in the eyes of the townsfolk and the orthodox. The expression "beyond the pale" carries the same anxieties. "Pale" is the Old English word for fence or wall. So anything "beyond the pale" is unacceptable, beyond tolerating, or worse.

Though conversion was still the order of the day in Christian Europe, the old tribal memory persisted, and according to that, the Other was implacably disowned and money was still used to disavow and segregate him or her. This instinct to disavow and hide away the discredited parts of the self is common in individuals and across whole cultures. Today in the psychological world, the phenomenon is called splitting. Inside European cultures, moral and civil law, spiritual and secular activities, Brother and Other, were split off from each other, and the division was masked by the religious overlay that vindicated usury.

The third epoch of usury in Western culture was brought in around the time of Luther. The ecclesiastical Reformers courted serious and widespread social revolution by breaking allegiance with Rome, but they maintained stability by preserving Roman civil law and supporting the emerging merchant princes. In a movement that presaged the eventual fate of Indigenous peoples in the Americas, European peasants were obliged to surrender their collective wealth to the merchant princes by surrendering their collectively owned lands and resources, and they were turned into tenant farmers. The Roman law was invoked by the princes as justification because "the Roman law knew only private property . . . [and another] change was the substitution of exchange in coin for exchange in kind."[4]

The struggle over usury at this point was no longer one of separating sacred money from profane money. It said: there is only money. The chasm between the sacred and the profane was in each person's soul. Luther psychologized usury and this division between Brother and Other by bringing the sacred-profane split out of the tribal or political arena and proposing that it lay *inside each person.*

> Now *each man* is divided. The church and the state may
> be separate but each man partakes of both. When each man
> has a civil and a moral part, the brother and the stranger live
> side by side in his heart. Now when I meet someone on the
> street he is either alien or kin, *depending on his business*
> [italics mine].[5]

In Protestant Reformation thought, the inevitability of usury was not seriously challenged, because it was something justified and defended by state or secular law. The only question left was, Who is going to do it to whom? Forbidden to exact interest on loans by the old taboo of defilement and dislocation from the tribe, the Christian by and large handed these functions over to the Jew, the outsider. Given the edgy outsider status which Jews in the diaspora of mediaeval Europe endured, usury would have had a very practical aspect. As a business, it had no inventory and allowed for high mobility — a necessity in times of persecution, banishment, or forced conversion. Usury also required considerable education, social savvy, and business acumen, merits which were probably reluctantly acknowledged most — if at all — by the burghers, nobles, and merchants who used their services.

The problems surrounding money had become so confounding by this period that money itself came to be regarded as toxic stuff, and it had all the fatal attraction and aura of the forbidden. This attraction was mediated by the Jew. In other words, the Jew was used by secular Christian Europe to handle the functions of usury as tongs or robotic arms would be used to handle toxic, radioactive material. The history of usury is also the history of avoiding contamination by making use of a "necessary'" evil, and this entailed investing a sense of filth and contagion in those who handled it. All of the anthropological thinking concerning ritual defilement on a societal scale is applicable here.

Money can mean anything, and no fixed significance can be given to money's volume. A meagre amount could be good or bad, depending. Spiritually minded people are less inclined to ascribe the same imprecision, or neutrality, to a pile of money, for generally in those circles it is a bad thing: the more money, the worse for its keeper. This is not a new misgiving in spiritual circles: Martin Luther didn't hesitate over it. In 1566 he wrote, "Wealth is the smallest thing on earth, the least gift that God has bestowed on mankind." His stand is a little soft where he calls it "the least gift," considering the subject and Luther's general inclination to declare himself clearly, but he does offer this grim and satisfied observation, lest the parishioner or the reader harbour any doubt about money and the spiritual life:

> Wealth has in it neither material, formal, efficient, nor final cause, nor anything else that is good; therefore our Lord God commonly gives riches to those from whom he withholds spiritual good.[6]

So, it is one or the other for Luther. He has no tolerance for the dilemmas money poses for a person concerned with God and the religious and moral questions. He declares clearly that money condemns the spiritual person to misery and to separation from God, and that money and spirituality will never be found together. Luther is ruthless in his rigid, literal devastation of money's many faces, making them unrecognizable and indistinguishable, one from the other. He flattens money and sees only menace. There is no courage in his contemplation. God, he says, punishes people by making them rich. Money is a heaven-sent condemnation. This is a flat, unimaginative, and deeply naïve understanding, and it shows Luther's preference for authority over authenticity. Wherever the rich turbulence of life is reduced to an impoverished and simple choice of one thing over the other, you can be sure something intolerable has been stirred, and this poverty of choice disguises an effort to wrestle down, subdue, and slay this ambivalence. Aversions of this kind are confessions. Luther found darkness where he found money.

According to the Reformers of Luther's time, there are civil endeavours which are to be pursued civilly, and moral endeavours which are to be pursued morally, and they are not to be confused. Since the Brother and the Stranger live inside each person, and the Stranger can no longer be kept outside the city walls, usury might then be the entitlement of the civil or secular part of anyone who can gainfully pursue it. Here is Luther's understanding of the inevitability of inequity and the secular necessity of usury:

> Why is it that [Moses] permits repayment of a loan to be demanded from a stranger . . . but not from a brother . . . ? The answer is that this . . . is according to a just principle of public order, that by some privilege citizens are honoured beyond outsiders and strangers, lest everything be uniform and equal. While before God there is no respect of persons, but all are equal, yet in the world respect of persons and inequality are necessary.[7]

And elsewhere he wrote:

> The Jews do well obediently to yield themselves to God as instruments and to fulfill his wrath on the Gentiles through interest and usury.[8]

• • •

Strangely, and sadly, tracing the dance of usury and brotherhood through the ages, we find that as the circle defining brotherhood grew larger, the circle of trust grew smaller. That circle of trust shrank from a faith in the binding relationships of the clan or the tribe down to a measured calculation of the risks of personal relationships and of the trustworthiness of the Self and the Other. There was no assumption of a common God or a common good, no assumption of good will. Old-style kinship was irrelevant and the economics of scarcity drove the functions of money exchange between individuals. "After the sixteenth century," writes Hyde, "a brother is someone who will loan you money at the prime rate."[9]

The strain of this splitting off of the Other, and the psychological and spiritual turmoil it generated, has an accomplished witness in Shakespeare, whose play *The Merchant of Venice* still arouses the old ambivalences. It is too easy and too much to call Shakespeare an anti-Semite for having written this play. It is better to say that he is a witness who testifies to an age beset by this strain and describes it faithfully, which is more important than approving or disapproving of it. He deserves our gratitude as a witness whose story stirs our awareness of these things.

It is in the nature of psychological denial and repression, whether it be on an individual or a mass scale, that the unacknowledged thing — the demonized, disowned, split-off part of the self or the body politic — will return again and again in painful and tireless circles, usually compounded by the passage of time and the neglect that that entails. Principal and interest are here together: when the disowned part returns, you will not only have to contend with the principal, its demands and its chaos, all over again. You will also have to contend with the interest — the consequences of your neglect and disowning. Follow the trail that connects the anti-Pharisaism of the Gospel of John to the ambivalent fraternity of Mosaic and Christian theology in the writings of the early Church Fathers, to the Crusades and the Inquisition, to the *Merchant of Venice* and to the fantasies of tribal purity bred by National Socialism in Germany. That line describes the mythology that has grown up around the strange powers accruing to those engaged in the business of making and moving money, a mythology that was and is a kind of currency among those who look on the moneylenders with loathing.

Each generation can inherit countless evils from its forbears. Almost twenty years in the mental health game has persuaded me that we can inherit errors without end, and that old unconscious prejudices and malevolence can and do come into us as if through breastmilk; they come to us through casually overheard conversations between adults just as surely as they come to us through teaching and example. This grim inheritance is both willed and unconscious. But I have not yet seen that we can, with the same facility or inevitability, inherit enduring truths or life-giving or life-saving facts about love, or faithfulness, or kinship, or belonging. It seems that each of these truths must be forged anew by each generation.

The primitive and unacknowledged misgivings aroused by money tend to congeal around those who traffic in it. The history of usury, however, says more about monoculture tribalism than it says about money. Tribalism is a bad myth, and money has served this myth for millennia as a way of exorcising the stranger and maintaining some "purity" in the tribe. The longstanding enmity between Christian and Jewish myths of tribal identity, for instance, is a sad and emphatic example of this exorcism. Fear of the stranger and the demand that he worship the same God as you lies at the very root of usury.

There is another example available to us, a little more current. I am writing this in the first weeks after the September 11th bombings in New York and Washington. Most of the world has been dragged at a ragged and relentless pace from shock and disbelief to outrage, fear, and resignation about the darkness to come. A "new kind of war" has been declared by the American president against a faceless enemy he calls worldwide terrorism. For every American responding with anguished confusion about what America has done to be so hated, there might be ten thousand who condemn that kind of soul searching as unpatriotic and weak. The American president has simplified things for everyone: This was an attack on freedom. If you're not with us, you're with the terrorists. His is a literal, naïve, and fatal kind of tribalism.

In the midst of all this, against the odds, I am tremendously heartened to see a growing recognition among ordinary people that this kind of demented and heart-rending chaos comes in part from the inability of the North American tribe to see any kinship with the blighted and hope-deprived people in the Islamic tribe. Perhaps the same thing has happened in the Islamic world, and perhaps North Americans are only infinitely indulged and faceless foreigners to them. But inside this dark tunnel, there are some signs of a more compassionate awareness. Mosques in North America, for instance, have opened their doors and invited others in. The sounds of ecumenism that are stirring are aimed not just at curbing thuggish retaliations against North American Muslims. They are speaking to a deeper and misplaced fact: our own ancestral prejudices and our kinship with the diminished and the destitute on the other side of the world must be recognized and reclaimed and acted upon. North Americans have been visited by the inevitable consequences of our neglect of this crucial truth. In a world as small as this one, all people are kin. There can be no foreigner.

Money and Civilization

There must be something more to life
than having everything.
— MAURICE SENDAK

I read somewhere that Albert Einstein, toward the end of his life, was asked what his thoughts were about the ultimate reality of the universe. His reply: he wondered whether the universe was friendly or not. A cynic might suggest that this says something about the rigour of Einstein's thinking in his autumn years. But I love this story for the way it brings the limits of the most theoretical and imaginative rationalism into view. The teaching he gives here is subtle and perhaps self-effacing, but it is really a teaching about the Somewhere Else which his lifelong work in theoretical physics may have hinted at but did not bring him to.

The great physicist's life work was a kind of raid on the

inarticulate, to paraphrase T.S. Eliot. The program of ever-expanding rational knowledge and demythologization, over the last century in particular, appears to have pushed back the boundaries of the unknown to a point where humankind — Western humankind, at least — could seem almost self-sufficient. For about three centuries now, mystery increasingly appears to have given way to mastery, and Somewhere Else is getting farther and farther away.

In this chapter we'll track some of the mysteries of money up to the modern period. Specifically, we'll look at ways in which money and attitudes toward money have been used to subdue those who resisted money's most obvious "benefits." Money and the faith which accompanies it have for many centuries been used as agents of "civilization." Money has been a significant aspect of every program designed to civilize pagans, in both the Old World and the New. Money is a Great Power, and Money is a New Religion, particularly in the West. It has been inflicted on "primitive" people as one of the great gifts of the West. It's a strange choice for a rationalist culture to make, though, since money has so much magic and volatility in it. Foreboding and anxiety are aroused by the statelessness of money, by the suddenness and unruliness of its movements, and by the subtlety of its machinations. I think we should accept this as a fact as well as a fable. The ancients evidently sensed this, too, and were roused by its magic. This magic, this mercurial thing that is at once so common and so strange, seems to have only one foot in this world. The other foot is Somewhere Else.

The Orient has often superseded the Occident in matters of cultural sophistication; the implementation of paper money and the move toward face or symbolic value from inherent value was no exception. No less a mercantilist than Marco Polo made careful observation in the eleventh-century court of Kubla Khan of the almost exclusive use of paper money in the marketplaces. He marvelled at the sheer magical abstraction of money and at how the realm functioned smoothly by trafficking in this very symbolic way. Marco Polo was jolted to see the exponential leap in philosophy and sophistication from West to East, and the capacity for magical thinking that this revealed; the jolt was probably felt all the more for the fact that these achievements weren't yet even a rumour in Dark Age Europe. Marco Polo was awestruck by the civilization that paper money hinted at. The possibilities for exponential wealth which that symbolic value implied, another example of magical thinking, did not escape him either.

> The grand khan . . . may truly be said to possess the secret of the alchemists . . . The coinage [sic] of this paper money is authenticated with as much form and ceremony as if it were actually of pure gold or silver . . . All his subjects receive it without hesitation . . . Upon these grounds, it may certainly be affirmed that the grand khan has a more extensive command of treasure than any other sovereign in the universe.[1]

It is interesting that the khan exercised care to lavish ceremony upon the manufacture and circulation of paper money. It suggests there was an awareness in his court that the mythical elements money carried needed to be acknowledged and brought to conscious awareness. The rituals of authentication were surely an attempt to confer upon this paper abstraction the same *mysterium tremendum* that accrued to precious metals, and to invest them with symbolic value. Those rituals were an invitation extended to the Gods to mingle with money and with those who put their faith in its metaphorical powers. It was a wise gesture for an omnipotent ruler to guard against being totally carried away by his omnipotence by making room in the kingdom for the Gods of money.

In England in the seventeenth century, a number of measures were taken by the Treasury to stabilize the unsteady currency of the realm, including the release of new coinage. The results were more destabilizing, since many questions arose in the marketplace concerning the real precious metal content of the newly minted coins — hence the practice of biting coins to determine their fidelity. Many issues of coins were refused in trade. Mythologically speaking, this was because too much distance had opened up between their real value as objects cast of precious metal and their purported value in the marketplace, which was much more a question of symbol, consensus, and faith. Consensus value, even though guaranteed by the Crown and by the Treasury's gold holdings, was too slippery for trade and too slippery for trust. Consensus value was too magical. In other words, the coins had become too abstracted from their original inherent value, and their face value was too symbolic to be trusted. The subsequent introduction of paper money went even further in this direction and bred even greater anxiety, since there was no inherent value in printed paper at all. The irony is that the rationalist Enlightenment cultures of Europe were relying on money — magical, mythic, and inconstant — to carry the program of rationalism and civility.

Across the ocean almost a century later this dilemma persisted, and a lack of faith in paper currency bedevilled the new American federation of states. Thomas Jefferson, who as a successful mercantilist may have been a "player" in these matters, wrote in 1819 that

> the evils of this deluge of paper money are not to be
> removed, until our citizens are generally and radically
> instructed in their cause and consequences . . . Till then
> we must be content to return to the savage state, to recur to
> barter . . . for want of a stable, common measure of value,
> that now in use being less fixed than the beads and
> wampum of the Indian . . . [2]

I am sure Jefferson was hoping that such instruction would gather those in the marketplace into a new faith in the insubstantial currency. It was all uphill for him, though, because as the legacy of the Scientific Revolution and the Enlightenment worked its way through European culture, especially as it was transplanted to North America, the power of that legacy to challenge and ultimately to devastate mythological thinking made it harder, not easier, to sell money as the utter abstraction he imagined. When Jefferson lamented that the sophistication required to believe in abstraction was wanting in America, he spun an interesting web. Marco Polo, not touched by the pure rationalism that was to come, recognized (or was obliged to recognize) in the khan's rituals for paper money that cultural sophistication and making a place for the Gods go hand in hand. Jefferson, a son of the Enlightenment, could entertain no such "illusion." For him and his ilk, the Gods were savage and unsalvageable, whereas the abstraction of money was a pure and literal science. He saw the failure of faith in paper money as a kind of cultural regression to a pagan and savage state — the very thing from which money was supposed to deliver the new republic.

The modern era, really the whole of the time since the Enlightenment, has had to contend with this strange and faithless faith. Since then, money has fallen steadily into the realm of rumour, illusion, and shadow — out of the light. The last three centuries of Western culture have been spent trying to civilize or domesticate money and to wrestle it away from the Gods. Western culture has had to wrestle money, so to speak, with one hand tied behind its back, for Western culture is adamantly a demythologizing culture. Demythologization is a program fundamentally of desecration. One consequence is the annihilation of mystery. A demythologizing culture has a hard time with money, because fundamentally, money *is* mythological. A rationalistic, demythologizing culture has no conceptual vocabulary that might account for how magic does what it does. It loses its way of seeing such a thing at all. As English literary

61

scholar Dudley Young puts it, "If you want to traffic with the invisible, you have to use magic. Because we have forgotten this . . . we are . . . more ignorant of [the soul's desires] than were our primitive forbears."[3] The ignorance — and the neglect that ensues — carries tremendous consequence, as we saw in the last chapter.

Carl Jung, a student of Freud, felt the foreboding connected with money was justified, and reasoned that it was really a kind of recognition or acknowledgement of what money could do. Jung's view was that in human history *money brings the Gods to men*: When you contend with money, you contend with the Gods, too.

> Mercurius (the god of money), following the tradition of Hermes . . . is many-sided, changeable, and deceitful. (He is called) that inconstant Mercurius . . . He is *duplex* and his main characteristic is duplicity. It is said of him that he "runs around the earth and enjoys equally the company of the good and the wicked." He is "two dragons," the "twin," made of "two natures" or "two substances."[4]

Jung is saying that there is good reason for us to feel overpowered by money: it is God-like, but it is only like certain gods. James Hillman refers to Hermes as "the thief, patron of merchants, easy commerce."[5] Mythologically speaking, the character of the God reflects the functions of the money, and vice versa. Money lies outside the moral realm, like a God. It is no respecter of persons, and it will abide any company, a trait which brought considerable enmity Jesus' way, too. Money can fit right in, anywhere, and wreak havoc when it does.

The mediaeval alchemists used lead, a kind of brute substance that had no currency or value, as the raw material from which they sought to conjure or wrestle precious metal. It is not simply a silk purse from a sow's ear that the alchemist sought, not just an improvement or a refinement, as one of the processes of metallurgy is called today. The transmutation of lead into gold was *creation*, creation of the kind described in the book of Genesis. Alchemy was thought of as an ennobling enterprise, a raising-up process. It was *redemption* of a most profound kind, a redemption of brute matter, a transformation of shit into gold. The redemption the alchemist sought derived its worth in part from the extreme transformation from lower to higher, from earthly to heavenly — from lead to gold. W.H. Auden may just as well have been speaking of alchemists and of all the demythologizing culture of the West that takes its cue from Genesis and denies a soul to the world when he wrote this of Americans: their "great vice . . . is not materialism but a lack of respect for matter."[6]

The Indigenous peoples of Meso-America clearly attached value and importance to gold for its ornamental, symbolic, and aesthetic value, but they were nonetheless stunned by the Conquistador's madness for the accumulation of the stuff. It was madness to them because the soul in gold was not concentrated *only* in gold. There was soul in all of Creation. Alchemy, on the other hand, was an attempt to ennoble matter after the Gods had been driven from Creation and had become

63

mere rumours — after the world-soul had become a rumour.

Jung wrote that alchemists saw in base lead "something so bedevilled and shameless that all who wish to investigate it fall into madness through ignorance."[7] That's a strong indictment, and meant as fair warning to those who had some grasping naïveté about the magical process of creating wealth from "nothing." It surely attests to the toxic qualities attributed to the lurid fascination with making gold and wealth. What an unexpected attribute, though, to call lead "shameless"! It is a good way of revealing the moral overlay that shrouds monetary machinations, for this culture does not hesitate to attribute shame to a fascination with the making of money. Alchemy was about spiritualizing the dispirited. Perhaps it is too much to say that money is a spiritual thing, at least at this point in our discussion. What seems more than clear, though, is that money arouses the soul. It stirs the spirit pot. It is, without doubt, strong medicine. This is the kind of fact Olson was referring to when he wrote, "Moneys are facts to be dealt with," and to ignore it is to court "madness through ignorance."

Money has not lost any of its lustre. But it is a major undertaking to recognize the facts of money that we were thinking of earlier, particularly the mythological elements, in contemporary life. Here is a more current accounting of the accumulation of magic around the accumulation of money:

> To strike it rich . . . is something that has only become
> possible during the past century. Before mass industries
> sprang up, it was virtually unknown for a man to alter his

material circumstances by his efforts alone. He couldn't make money; it was granted him by a monarch or a war lord, or it came in the form of booty, or was taken out of the earth or conquered territory. But the alchemist's dream of creating wealth where there was none before, of conjuring it out of nothing, or out of something without known value, has only been realised in the last hundred years. The aggregate of all the world's millionaires throughout the whole of history up till 1875 is fewer than the number now to be found in the United States in any one year. It took the Krupps [Hitler's main munitions manufacturers] eight generations, starting in the sixteenth century, to obtain great wealth. By comparison Rockefeller did it in about forty years . . .[8]

• • •

It is hard to imagine a time in history when humans did not share the knowledge that we now have about the causal connection between copulation and procreation, but there was such a time. It certainly added to the mystery that gathered around conception and birth. It must have attributed fathomless generative power to the childbearer, and it probably relegated others — fathers in particular — to the status either of midwives or awed witnesses. Despite all of our anatomical knowledge to the contrary, much of this feeling of magic and otherworldly power still endures and rumbles out of the ancestral mists at conception and childbirth, and with the experience of falling in love — though the keepers of those mysteries tend now to be the geneticists, obstetricians, and psychologists.

Similarly, there was a time when humans did not think in terms of wealth being something we made, but rather something already extant, something discovered or stolen or inherited, something that was a given, something that was finite, growing on the hoof or sitting in the ground or hidden in a strong box somewhere. These days it is an unconscious and unexamined conviction that money is made, *ex nihilo*, and the keepers of the mysteries of making money are the economists and the market traders.

Somewhere in the last century or two something awakened and came forward, something that closely resembled what the alchemists had both feared and yearned after for generations. The discovery of it has released all the self-loathing, all of the "falling into madness through ignorance" that Jung fretted over. This oft-dreamt-of conjuring of something from nothing is now present in all our lives. Like all conjuring, it requires a certain faith in order to be seen. A special knowledge is needed to survive when in its presence, because there is madness afoot when it draws closer. In our time the prevailing faith is a faith in capital — not just in the acquisition of capital, but in the pure magic of capital itself. Faith in capital amounts to a faith in bounty without limit, unending increase, a free and unfettered flow of goods and services across all borders and ideologies . . . a real and present Garden of Eden. When free traders and monolithic world market hype masters sell their dreams to us, they are pitching something they believe is as natural and inevitable as a well-tended garden.

The dark magic that has released that conjuring power now

goes by the name of The Multiplier Effect. Being no economist, I can't pretend to understand the mechanics of the market-place, but that may not be necessary to grasp the idea. In a phrase, The Multiplier Effect explains how money can breed money, from itself. The cognoscenti call this interest, the *springing up of exponential increase*, where there was only a base element — principal — before. One of the great exegetes of the Gospel of Money is John Kenneth Galbraith, and he has described succinctly what is required for an economic system and a way of life based on this miraculous generativity: The structure depends on wants being created by the process by which they are satisfied.[9]

Of course, this simple and ingenious formula has been courted by all advertising people and by demagogues of all stripes. The accruing of interest requires *want* on the other end of the line. The awakening of the desire for more is the enabler. The miracle of interest generates its own necessity: we *should* have more because we *can* have more. I remember once being part of a discussion at a rich man's table. The question was whether a developer should be permitted to build a house in a particular ravine that was a source of visual and recreational pleasure for the community, and which was also a home for animals and plants that, while not exotic or endangered, were well established there. The conclusion was divided along financial lines: among those at the table with money, the view was that the project should be approved, while those of moderate means thought the preservation of the ravine should prevail. The rationale given by the well-to-do:

the builder should be allowed to do so because he can afford to do so. To their minds, the capacity provided by money to get the job done also conferred merit on the project at hand. There was no question as to whether it *should* be done, only whether it *could* be done, including whether there was enough money. This is an example of the enabler at work.

Galbraith's cogent observation about the need-making system might sound logical and inevitable to those of us who have grown from the womb with this system in place all around them, but it is better to think of it as *magic logic.* When it works, it works like a kind of miracle, like manna falling from heaven. When the miracle of wealth that comes from want does its work on us, as it does with merciless efficiency in the West, there is no decision making needed or invited. Having fallen under the spell of consumer market fundamentalism, people convince themselves that they need only what the market can give them. The process has a kind of *perfect* geometry about it. The longing in the human soul for security and abundance is aroused and satisfied again and again in mad and blind repetition by the ridiculous bounty and barely limited availability of consumer goods in the West. Ask any recent immigrant to the West from a former Soviet bloc country if this is true, and listen to how the sheer volume of available stuff intoxicated and bewitched them when they were first exposed to it. When they can afford it, they are some of the West's best consumers.

Lewis Hyde has written, "The desire to consume is a kind of lust. We long to have the world flow through us like air or food. Consumer goods merely bait this lust, they do not satisfy it."[10] In other words, the sparse limitations on availability remove necessity, purpose, advisability, and wisdom, and provoke in their place a naked, hard-to-recognize and easily misconstrued longing for *more*. That longing is, perhaps strangely to some, almost unbearable. I have seen more incidents of outright child abuse in large supermarkets than I have heard of in my office, and this is why. The supermarket, with its aisles of pleasure and unleavened, unrestricted bounty, seduce this longing in everyone to some degree, but emphatically in children, for whom the business of paying at the checkout is but a trifling, momentary delay of gratification. Their wanting is most naked. The fact that the child acts on this longing by grabbing, chewing, demanding, and crying for things drives many parents, who are also prone to the same anxiety that comes from exposure to this kind of excess, to blatant and regrettable excesses of their own. What we parents experience through our children, we usually blame on our children. We blame the kids for giving too much voice to the longing that is stirred up in them, and for being too faithful to it, and for stirring it up in us. The signs on the bulk-food store bins say NO SNACKING, but they really mean NO WANTING THAT MUCH.

The consumer of commodities is invited to a meal without passion, a consumption that leads to neither satiation nor fire. He is a stranger seduced into feeding on the drippings of someone else's capital *without benefit of its inner nourishment*, and he is hungry at the end of the meal, depressed and weary as we all feel when lust has dragged us from the house and led us to nothing. A restless hunger springs up when the gift is not being eaten [italics mine].[11]

That sounds like an average kind of shopping trip to me. I am *sure* that there is nourishment for the soul to be had from mingling with capital, but the arousal of the longing for more, and the seduction of interest, particularly when it remains unconscious, is not nourishing at all. It is seduction, not courtship. It offers something, but only to get something more in return.

When you are in the world of making money, "not having enough" is no longer a description of a subjective state, negotiable and resolvable. They say you can never have too much. So "not having enough" is an imperative, not a decision. It rouses a part of the self which feels bereft, and this aroused and demented self moves off, nosing the breeze with a faintly menacing, faintly desperate air, in the direction of someone else's surplus or plenitude or achievement. And "never having enough" necessarily has as its corollary "the inexhaustible source," the Garden. This means that whenever the feeling of not being secure with what you have comes forward, the presumption that there is a surplus Somewhere Else, which can be obtained to remove this feeling of inadequacy, is close at hand. These things should be recognizable to us by now: *they are very close in spirit to the longing for a sense of God-in-the-world.* Money's provenance is mythological and archaic, and it has a kinship with the divine and the holy and the Other

World. The Multiplier Effect describes that kinship, without intending to. The fact that one can grow wealthy from the spiritual longing of others is not something that has occurred only to the televangelists. It is the Holy Grail in advertising and a fact in the marketplace.

"The more we long for something, the more value do we attribute to the capacity to satisfy that longing, and therefore the more do we envy the person who has that capacity," says John Kenneth Galbraith.[12] Envy is an instinct as old as the ooze. It sounds harsh to call envy an instinct, since to do so seems to make envy inevitable whenever people are together. But envy endures, and it is not diminished by education or by bounty. It curls around the bedrock of human experience. It is among the most primitive of human emotions. That means envy has a powerful bypass mechanism accompanying it. As an instinct, it is driven by a feeling of necessity and a sense that one is subservient to it, and it is not subject to hesitation, doubt, or scrutiny. Its appearance on the scene *justifies* its existence. Envy brings back into economic life and spiritual life the feeling of necessity that had been temporarily blurred by the prospect of unbridled bounty. By necessity, I mean that inevitable feeling that you are suddenly unsure of yourself and your prospects because your neighbour, it turns out, has some of what is justly yours. Envy turns companionship into competition, with familiar results.

Sometimes I forget completely
what companionship is.

71

Unconscious and insane, I spill sad
energy everywhere. My story
gets told in various ways: A romance,
a dirty joke, a war, a vacancy.
Divide my forgetfulness to any number,
it will go around . . .[13]
— RUMI

When envy comes, the poet warns, there's always more than enough to go around. And at times like these, envy will be the only thing appearing in sufficient quantity to be shared. Envy brings its own economics, an economics which is simple and compelling: if you have some (or appear to have some) and I have little or none or not enough (or feel as though I do), then you must have some of mine. If I have three and you have seven, you have two — at least two — of mine. There is only so much to go around (the assumption of scarcity being fundamental in this system), and you have what I am missing. This is a simple extension of the principal that came up earlier: my sense of inadequacy carries the fantasy of limitless surplus somewhere on its back. If that feeling of inadequacy persists, it must be because the surplus is lost or misplaced somewhere — or is being withheld by someone. Anyone who sees things in this way sullenly resents this withholding because they experience it as punitive, and they envy the bounty they imagine the "withholding one" has.

So envy can endure any demonstration of fairness or equity and come out intact. It depends not on the facts of the distribution of wealth, but on a sense of grievance and inadequacy, feelings which are pervasive and often implacable. This was made plain to me when a rich man described to me the way he chooses his friends. "I only have a few," he said, "and I make sure that they have *at least* as much money as I do, and can afford to do *at least* those things that I can afford to do." While at the time I thought that this was unnecessarily insular and elitist and the very recipe for an impoverished inner life, I saw later that he was speaking about his own experience of this implacable envy in others, and with some wisdom had decided that there was nothing to be done. He, too, believed that envy bedevils human instinctual life and intimate life — so much so that there is no peace where money and relationship meet. So he appealed to money as the great arbiter of justice: if you have enough to run with me, then you are entitled to run with me. Otherwise, you are not. I saw several businessmen join with him during the boom years of the mid-1980s in hopes of being similarly blessed by the Gods of commerce. Without the resources to run with him, however, they were all burnt in the comet trail of his success, and fell in the slowdown at the end of the decade. The gnashing of teeth, which is envy made audible, accompanied the fall.

• • •

The presence of money in any human story helps to reveal the prevailing attitudes about private possession, gifting, and sharing. These attitudes give a broad band of information about what a culture values in a person, what it values in a possession, and they reveal its convictions about the nature of personhood and brotherhood. It continues to come as a shock to many Anglo North Americans to learn that other cultures do not regard money, possessions, ownership, and sharing with the same automatic responses as we do. The First Nations of this continent certainly had other ideas about these things.

When Europeans first encountered Indigenous peoples in the Caribbean and up along the Atlantic coast, and for a long while afterwards, they did not recognize them as humans. To the Europeans they hardly looked human, in an anatomical way, and they clearly didn't act human. Slowly and reluctantly and guardedly over the subsequent decades, the Europeans — later to become the North Americans — conceded the approximate humanity of Indigenous peoples, but they continued to insist that they lacked something which was a more fundamental requirement. Indigenous peoples, they said, may have had the biology of humanity, but they didn't have the civilization of humanity. The proof? They didn't know how to value things.

Except for items for immediate personal or ritual use, First Nations people tended to hold most property in common. Gift giving was an essential part of communal ownership. It guaranteed the continued movement of goods through the community, and it created and sustained and secured relationships between people and between tribal groups. The *Huron Relation of 1635*, a sort of year-in-review written by the Jesuit Jean de Brébeuf during his tenure with the Huron in present-day Ontario, contains several observations about these practices. In one case, Brébeuf describes how fire had swept through a village twice in a year, and how the same man's house had been spared both times. This man's response was to feed the village by giving away much of his surviving food stores until the people were able to fend for themselves again. Brébeuf, his jaundiced eye firmly fixed on the scene, noted that the man's charity was a calculating example of enlightened self-interest: "The act appeased them . . . This was prudent to lose one portion in order to keep the other." Brébeuf was a good Jesuit, and he saw himself and all Europeans as the crown of Creation, made in the image of the European God. Naturally, he speculated, God had spared this man's house because he had given a kind welcome to Brébeuf and the other missionaries of Christian civilization.

Elsewhere in the *Relation*, Brébeuf writes that he was shocked to find that "even the most avaricious among . . . [the Hurons] spare nothing. We have seen some of them practically stripped of all their goods, because several of their friends had died, to whose souls they had made gifts." There was no ownership without the sharing of bounty, good fortune, or bare necessity between people, and between the living and the dead.

They have some remarkable moral qualities [wrote Brébeuf].

We notice, foremost, a great love and bond for each other, which they are careful to develop by marriage, by gifts, by their feasts . . . When they come back from fishing, hunting,

and their trading, they share a great deal with one another.
If they have something special, even if they have bought it
or it has been given to them, they make a feast for the
whole village. Their hospitality to every manner of stranger
is noteworthy . . . They give the best of what they have . . .
I do not know whether anything to equal this can be
found elsewhere.[14]

By "elsewhere," of course, the Jesuit meant Europe, or civilization, or humanity. Brébeuf can't help himself; though he
viewed them as savages and pagans and devil worshippers,
they seemed to know something about value, possessions, and
brotherhood that worked, something that Europeans had no
notion or memory of. The Aboriginal capacity for social organ-
ization, of which gift giving was an integral part, posed a great
challenge to the European inclination to believe that the only
humans were European humans, and the only property was
private property.

Even though these gift-giving practices were under constant
attack, they survived in many Aboriginal jurisdictions well into
the nineteenth century. A "civilized" Sioux man from present-
day Minnesota, whose white name was George Eastman,
recalled that

public giving is part of every important ceremony. It properly
belongs to the celebrations of birth, marriage, and death, and
is observed whenever it is desired to do special honour to
any person or event. Upon such occasions it is common to

76

give to the point of utter impoverishment. The Indian literally gives away all that he has, to guests of another tribe or clan, but above all to the poor and the aged, from whom he can hope for no return.[15]

By the early nineteenth century, Anglo North America was a spawn of mercantile capitalism, and it howled with the unrequited appetite, the unbridled yearning, for more. Monolithic and single-minded, it demanded more space, more land, more resources, more of what it knew, more of what it was. There was, however, one obstacle in the way of the technology driven advancement of civilization: First Nations peoples continued to stubbornly occupy what little was left of the "New World." They also, with greater or lesser success, stubbornly resisted being civilized. So wherever military annihilation, disease, starvation, and appropriation of lands did not exterminate or remove them, a policy of assimilation was undertaken — extermination by other means. One common plank in the platform of assimilation adopted by the American and the Canadian governments was the termination of all Aboriginal beliefs and practices with respect to public and private wealth and the distribution of goods. By this time there was little sign of Brébeuf's marvelling at the gift giving and generosity of Aboriginal peoples. Instead, what was left of the Indigenous peoples were seen merely as examples of primitive ignorance and a lack of social and intellectual sophistication. Money and attitudes about ownership and property were the blunt end of the club used to impress upon them the supposedly undeniable, irresistible, and inevitable merits of civilization.

It is fascinating and sadly instructive to see the sheer moral outrage aroused in businesspeople and legislators of the sovereign culture when they were faced with the Aboriginal person's reluctance to embrace the "obvious" benefits of the market economy, private ownership of lands, and faith in money's abstracted value. Dr. Merrill Gates, an American who described himself as a "Friend of the Indians," wrote something along those lines at the wane of the nineteenth century:

> To bring the Indian out of savagery into citizenship we
> need to awaken in him wants. In his dull savagery *he must
> be touched by the wings of the divine angel of discontent* . . .
> Discontent with the teepee and the Indian camp . . . is
> needed to get the Indian out of the blanket and into trousers
> — and trousers with a pocket in them, and with a pocket
> that aches to be filled with dollars! *Here is an immense
> moral training that comes from the use of property.* Like a
> little child who learns the true delight of giving away only
> by first earning and possessing what it gives, the Indian
> must learn that he has *no right to give until he has earned,*
> and that he has no right to eat until he has worked for his
> bread. Our teachers upon the reservations know that
> frequently their lessons . . . are effaced and counteracted
> by the Indians' old communal instincts and customs. We
> have found it necessary, as one of the first steps in develop-
> ing a stronger personality in the Indian, to make him

responsible for property. Even if he learns its value only by losing it, and going without it until he works for more, the educational process has begun [italics mine].[16]

Gates' proposal for the First Nations peoples raises a deep question, one that he presumed and argued for, but didn't ask: When is a person a person? What is the root conviction in the West about personhood? And what would qualify an Indian to be a person? Anglo-American culture demanded that Indigenous peoples would have to turn away from their extended family and their neighbours, turn away from their clan and their tribal affiliations. The nuclear family would be their only material and moral responsibility, and that family would mark the boundary of their kinship. They would have to stop sharing and start owning, stop giving away and start hoarding. They would have to believe in enlightened self-interest. They would have to develop contempt for the have-nots. They needed a good dose of self-reliance, self-confidence, self-directedness — all of them recipes for self-absorption, all of them aimed at melting the relationships between kin and between tribes. Only then would the Indigenous person be a human being, worthy of civilization. Gates is recommending that the Indians' communal identity be broken, that the Indian be infantilized and turned toward self-absorption as a prerequisite for becoming a good citizen and a good consumer. In Anglo North America, they're the same thing.

The hard, dull, yellowed eye of Western capital culture

looked down upon the communal property ownership and the distribution of wealth in Indigenous cultures and saw only a doomed and uncivilized attempt to control the individual urge toward hoarding, meanness, and social chaos. Freud viewed any "civilizing" instinct in similar terms — that is, it was an attempt to control self-satisfying and savage anarchic impulses. The "savages of the New World" developed communal ownership as a highly prized social value which created and sustained both individual identity and cultural cohesion. This achievement seems to have made almost no impression on the civilization overwhelming them, and it did nothing to soften the civility inflicted upon them.

It is grimly fascinating to see how the addiction to individual ownership of property and the market economy utterly blinded the Anglo-American mind to this Aboriginal practice and to the merits of communal ownership. Gates' claim is that the capacity to share must be earned by serving the self first, just as the "right" to eat must be earned by making money to buy one's food. Gates' insistence that giving is a kind of entitlement that can be bought only by being ensnared by self-interest is heartbreaking in a way. Colonizing prejudices such as these annihilated a human achievement that was ritually profound and beautiful, rooted in mythological thinking and in serving the human, animal, and spirit worlds — and replaced it with social and spiritual poverty. Those so prejudiced assured themselves then — and still do — that their approach was pedagogy and not imperialism, compassion and not oppression.

Gates' admonition reflects the Gospel of Consumer Culture. This gospel is current. It is not dated and embarrassing cultural insensitivity. The manufacture of desire and the assumption of the universal attraction to, and the necessity for, a uniform market economy is the cornerstone of the tidal wave of globalization that is now sweeping across all Western and many non-Western countries. Gates' vision and the vision of globalization are the same: the perfectibility of humankind through baptism in the marketplace. The gross intolerance for local diversity and the adamant insistence upon monoculture and standardization — achieved through invoking global markets, products, and procedures — continues to be a hallmark of Western civilizing of the Indigenous world.

The widespread practice of give-aways in the Pacific Northwest is well known. It survived contact with European culture until the late nineteenth century, and in the last half of the twentieth century was being practised again. It is called potlatch, and it often marked important moments in personal and tribal life, such as the anointing of a new chief. The person who gave the potlatch would work for a considerable time, gathering large amounts of local products and trade goods. During the ceremony, the celebrant would distribute these things to the people, until he or she was destitute. That person's poverty was one sign of a well-done potlatch. The ceremony was part of an elaborate social system of gift circulation that established status and material and spiritual well-being all at the same time. Materially, the potlatch reinforced the circulation of commodities by turning them into gifts. Spiritually, the ceremony continually raised people up and reduced them, and it bred humility and gratitude in giver and receiver.

The local governments were scandalized by the notion of voluntary impoverishment, and saw the potlatch as an impediment to the acquisition of civilization. To the white authorities the custom was a moral outrage, for they saw in it a lack of respect for ownership and material goods, and a lack of respect for the work and sacrifice they represented. It is not difficult to see, however, that *respect for possession* lay at the heart of the potlatch. Giving away was the key element in ownership, the key ingredient in social status. The value of material goods was established and reiterated not by keeping them, but by giving them away, and their face value grew by being given away — a beautiful and useful logic that utterly evaded the authorities.

By the end of the last century, however, the potlatch tradition had been severely corrupted by the availability of cheap, poorly made European trade goods and by the war waged upon communal ownership by European traders, local colonial administrators, and missionaries. The things given away at potlatch had lost much of their old face value. Their easy availability, the fact that they were no longer tied directly to labour and to traditional ways of gathering or preparation, devalued them and multiplied them simultaneously. The result was often a rivalry in the display of this voluntary impoverishment. The potlatch of the late nineteenth century was the progeny of a European capitalism mated to an Aboriginal gift economy, with freakish results: sewing machines thrown into the sea, people embarrassed into sitting in houses set afire with fish oil, Indians dancing with pink silk parasols or stooped under layer after layer of cheap wool blankets, and the RCMP riding off with coppers and other ritual property to suppress the potlatch, which their government had declared illegally wasteful.[17]

When rituals lose contact with the spiritual facts of daily life and become only symbolic, and when material necessity and tradition no longer have any part to play, they turn into dense, desolate effigies and idols, and they speak not to what has survived — if anything — but to what has been lost.

Communal ownership and free circulation of goods among Aboriginal people galled white administrators. When their wrath was calmed into pity, it sounded like this observation from the late-nineteenth-century American Senator Dawes:

The head chief told us that there was not a family in that whole nation that had not a home of its own. There was not a pauper in the nation, and the nation did not owe a dollar . . . Yet the defect of the system was apparent. They have got as far as they can go, because they own their land in common . . . There is no enterprise to make your home any better than that of your neighbour's. There is no selfish-ness, which is at the bottom of civilisation. Until this people consent to give up their lands and divide them among their citizens so that each can own the land he cultivates, they will not make much progress.[18]

This is a gospel so monumental and monolithic in its arrogance, so irredeemable and so unreflective that the imagination shudders in the presence of it. And yet in its time (and its time may not be past), it was no doubt seen as compassionate and inclusive. If you sniff this over, though, you may catch, under the sneering disgust and the patronizing superiority, the telltale odour of envy. When I read this, I remembered being at an Ojibwa pow-wow, where the dancers flew in beautiful circles and raised the dust up over the arbour as the drums carried their feet. The extravagant pride of appearance and performance somehow ennobled all who were there. The announcer said that the Anishnabe tradition was a prophetic one, and that the prophecy had been given that there would be signs of the end of the First Nations' seven generations of suffering, and that one sign would be the growing envy of whites for what Indians had not forgotten.

Lest there be any melancholy over the passing of Aboriginal wisdom concerning wealth and community, we should bear in mind that Aboriginal people have endured considerable trespass and are still among us, and we should be aware that there are living traditions of wisdom about gifting and sharing, hoarding and self-absorption that are still practised and taught. In some Aboriginal circles, miraculously, there is even a willingness to share some of this wisdom with white society, as a gift.

• • •

When is a culture a culture? What qualities make a nation? Not too long ago, Canadians had a good encounter with the moral force of Aboriginal teachings on power, personhood, and nationhood. In 1982, then-Prime Minister Pierre Trudeau repatriated all constitutional powers from England to Canada. In doing so, he was attempting to grow the country, finally, beyond its colonial adolescence.

In the course of the wrangling and deal-making that ensued, the old, implacable divisions between English and French Canada came round again, and then-Premier of Québec, René Lévesque, withdrew from the process. In 1989, then-Prime Minister Brian Mulroney tried taking the next step toward nationhood by negotiating a new power-sharing scheme between the provinces and the federal government. A key element of the deal was Québec's insistence that the new scheme recognize historical and cultural fact by acknowledging Québec as a distinct society.

One of many legal requirements of the process was that all provinces vote unanimously for the measure through their individual legislatures. Surely, the popular wisdom went, every elected provincial politician would declare him or herself in favour of such a natural, easy-to-support proposal. And every one did, until a little-known member of the Manitoba Legislature named Elijah Harper, an Aboriginal man, in consultation with his elders, voted no. And the seemingly inevitable slide toward rubberstamped full nationhood stopped there. The process had failed to recognize an older, deeper fact from the prehistory of the country: Canada had been achieved at the expense of, and in spite of, its Aboriginal peoples. "Canada" was the story of winners. The federal and provincial governments had again proceeded as if this were not so. Whatever Harper's personal or tribal motivations may have been, the echo in the country's soul was clear, unromantic, and mature: you cannot have a country, and you cannot be initiated into soulful, authentic maturity as a nation, until the old habits have been sacrificed. In this case, that means an end to the continued diminishment of the status of First Nations peoples and the need to recognize and redress the insane harm done to those nations in the name of civilization, the consequences of which endure and proliferate to this day. It was an initiation which in many ways, the creation of Nunavut notwithstanding, the country continues to avoid.

Money in Men's Lives

Many men go fishing all of their lives without knowing that it is not fish they are after.
— HENRY DAVID THOREAU

Here is a story about a man of moderate means. His wife was several months pregnant at the time of their wedding. He was genuinely happy with both the pregnancy and the wedding, but his frail contentment prepared him not at all for a very brief conversation he had at the reception. In a quiet moment he was approached by his new brother-in-law, who put his arm comfortably around the man's shoulders and came unexpectedly and squarely to the point. "You know," the brother-in-law began, "it's funny how things change. Twenty-five years ago I would've broken both your legs. Now, I give you five Gs as a wedding present." There was no irony, no sarcasm. Just the news. He smiled, he squeezed the man's shoulders with what might have been a kind of affection, and he walked away.

For people with a nose for menace, it's a disquieting little story. It's certainly a good introduction to the present theme of how money and masculinity are woven together. At first blush the brother-in-law seems to be making a harsh but maybe innocent joke about how times have changed, and how family honour and chivalry are measured a little differently now. But I think there is a darker notice being given to the groom, something that has nothing to do with changes in social convention, something like the primitive anarchy we found in the Creation myth. The brother-in-law is, to be genteel, engaging in a bit of anatomy comparison. The groom is being told that his paternity is yet to be established, because real masculinity comes from where the money comes from. The brother-in-law, whatever his motivations, has it figured out. He is saying, "Copulating with my sister is one thing, my friend. Marrying, too. But being the man, being the father — for that, you're going to need money you might never have. Don't think otherwise." The groom is well advised: Around here the money makes the man.

The idea of masculinity has endured many insults, challenges, revisions, and dismissals over the last forty years. It's hard to use the word "masculine" and not draw uneasiness and suspicion from all sides. Our job in this chapter will be to wonder how a man's relationship to men of his generation and of other generations — and a man's relationship to himself — has become as troubled as it is in our time. The role that money plays in establishing and diminishing maturity and masculinity, and the way it confounds different generations of men differently, will be our particular focus. No doubt, what follows will not apply well or equally to all men, and it isn't intended to. But if you don't recognize any personal dilemma here, chances are that you know several men for whom these dilemmas could be true. This material might help to understand those men a little better, and you might be able to offer a little help to them. So we'll begin by picking up a theme that appeared briefly in the last chapter: when does a person become a person in our culture? Then we'll get to the money.

Most cultures the world over, and Indigenous cultures in particular, practise some kind of ritual personmaking. They seem to agree that persons are made, not born. But there are vast differences between cultures in how that personmaking happens, and as many differences in how one is judged to have become a person. As the dominant culture in North America has grappled with the ethical morass of reproductive technologies and abortion, it has tended to rely on legal definitions of personhood, and it has tried to articulate and advocate the value of the human being by placing personhood as close to conception as biology and the microscope will allow. However, the real gold standard for emotional and intellectual identity and health in the West — what this culture would mean by personhood — is not conception or birth, but the achievement of what psychology calls individuation. Individuation is offered up as the prerequisite accomplishment which qualifies a person to be a person. In the West, a developing psyche must define itself against the nurturing culture.

The tension between being one's self and belonging to others appears in different ways at different stages prior to adulthood. The specifically adolescent variety of individuation requires rebellion against the parent and the culture that the parent represents, and it is the hallmark of emerging personhood. Simply put, personhood is achieved, at least initially, by saying no and by turning away. This leads to all kinds of dilemmas later in life, because it never quite becomes clear when saying yes and turning toward someone and "losing yourself" in an intimate relationship or in a cause is desirable or necessary. Individuation is a turning toward the self. But it is also an uncertain business, because it begs the questions: what self, and where does it come from? Turning away from parents is clear enough, but how is one to turn toward a self not yet realized? Without much of an answer from the popular culture, people accept this as a universal necessity and truth without hesitation, and imagine that cultures the world over do this — or should. We comfort ourselves by reassuring each other that this individuation is pretty much a given, an inevitability. We count on it to happen, without focusing too much concern on how it happens, or whether it happens, or what is to be done if it doesn't happen.

There are other cultures, cultures not fundamentally unhinged by contact with the Western rationalist tradition, which have practised or continue to practise a much different kind of personmaking. Most adolescent rites of passage in Indigenous cultures, for example, aim for an annihilation of the strong and tenacious attachment to one's childhood that one carries into adolescence, and this is key for achieving personhood. In this context, personhood is something achieved with great effort and sacrifice. Through such processes as gender segregation, scarification, and extended ritual initiation by elders other than one's own parents, these cultures turn the initiate away from the self. This means turning away from childhood preoccupations with comfort and familiarity, away from self-absorption, and toward the language and ways of the soul, toward attachment to ancestors and elders and service to the community. In these cultures, attachment to the self is seen as a vestige of childhood ways, and it is believed to interfere with deep participation in spiritual and cultural life. The surrender of self-absorption — and it is an unwilling surrender — is a prerequisite for soulful personhood in these cultures.

• • •

I have often wondered at the rites of passage — really the remnants of those rites — that we hold on to in this culture, and I've wondered whether these rituals do what we hope they do. My contemplation on this point was triggered years ago when I began to notice that I was seeing many, many men who showed most or all of the markers of success and accomplishment our culture uses to indicate the achievement of personhood, but who were utterly undone by the complexities of intimacy and the struggle to nurture a soulful sensibility in their lives. Typically, many of them were reduced to being petulant, withdrawn, and wounded adolescents by failure and loss in intimacy, though they were forty or fifty years old. And I had to wonder, What use is all their expertise if it doesn't translate into making sense of these miseries? How is it that all those accomplishments don't translate into something approaching wholeness, or personhood?

Years ago I heard an anecdote attributed to Carl Jung. If it is not an accurate story, it should be. "If I am forced to choose," Jung is supposed to have said, "I would rather be whole than be good." You could argue that it is an old man's prerogative to make such fine and theoretical distinctions, but I see it as an old man's experience talking. This is to my mind an exceptionally wise choice that Jung advocates. Jung is saying that goodness is more than good intent or adequate accomplishment, that there is no capacity for goodness without wholeness, and that wholeness is more than competence and goodness. If people, whole people, can be recognized by their ability to live deeply and thoroughly, with mystery and ambiguity intact, and if that wholeness is also evident in their struggles and frailties and abject failures, then personhood may not be as common or inevitable an achievement as this culture presumes — or hopes — it is.

I wonder if our rituals really aim to make a whole person. Most of them appear to *guarantee* passage to wholeness, rather than providing a way of attaining it. There is no risk, no mayhem, no danger, no loss in the rituals — in fact, they seem intent on *saving* us from those experiences — and there is very little substance to the symbolism they rely upon. We tend to replace those trials with small doses of performance anxiety. Is it possible, for example, to fail your First Communion or your Bar Mitzvah? Is anyone sent back to work harder and hope for another chance? We all know a child who has been passed into the next grade, even though he or she did not achieve the necessary results for moving on. We all know this was done in order to spare the child a sense of failure, futility, or shame. But what else are they spared? What are the consequences of this phantom achievement? Well, the child did not taste ignominy, certainly, and that seems compassionate, but what else did he or she not taste? When is the achievement a real one?

It seems to me that if the possibility of failure is absent, if you don't risk not attaining that passage into the next necessary stage of your life, and if there is no loss, particularly the loss of the security and familiarity that childhood clings to, then the ritual is an empty cup. This makes a painful question clear: How do you know when you've become a person? Some time ago my son had his Bar Mitzvah. I listened carefully when the rabbi described what the ritual meant. I was, I admit, dismayed. There was no mention of adulthood or manhood. Maybe, though, that omission was an honest one. Maybe the service and the readings and the party afterwards didn't by themselves turn him into a human being, and the rabbi was acknowledging that. Months later, my son told me that at first his only purpose in going throu gh the exercise was to get the presents and the money. But he'd come to realize that he'd wrestled with some fears he'd had, and he felt he'd achieved something for himself by doing so. He seemed with hindsight to have found a nose for the challenge, and he might have wrung something of the real trauma from the domesticated ritual.

What happens in a culture that has this kind of confusion around maturity and personhood? What becomes of the relationships between the generations when personhood is reduced to, "Hey, whatever works for you"? In his good and important book, *The Sibling Society*, Robert Bly looks at how the discrediting of one's own parents usually becomes a discrediting of parenthood, and then of adulthood per se. He describes a clear path to betrayal, a path that moves from the one who you feel has betrayed you to all of those who have betrayed you to the untrustworthiness of the world and into the face of God. After that kind of enmity sets in, there is no tolerance for the concept of accumulated wisdom, for tradition. The gradations of experience are flattened and worthless. There are no elders, there is no learning, no esteem, no praise or blessing. Instead of the vertical gaze into the face of the elder (which is where we learn how to gaze into the face of God), there are furtive sidelong glances into the face of the competitor, the sibling. In the absence of parents or elders, when the culture is flattened by this abandonment of the hard work of coming into adulthood, everyone is a sibling. Of course, the principal feeling tone among siblings in our culture is rivalry and envy. It is fuelled by a presumption of scarcity of emotional care and emotional food. It is shaded by an insipid

and insatiable longing for attention, which is the longing for an
elder or mentor gone awry.

As this dissolution drags on, there is no longer any feeling
that endurance of ambivalence, delayed gratification, grace
under pressure, discipline, or general goodness have any merit
at all. The living human examples of endurance, grace, and
goodness are too rare, and where they appear, they often look
like hapless saps and suckers and boobs. As Bly puts it:

> Adults regress toward adolescence; and adolescents —
> seeing that — have no desire to become adults. Few are
> able to imagine any genuine life coming from the vertical
> plane — tradition, religion, devotion. The Interior Judge
> remains authoritarian and brutal, but it no longer asks the
> citizen to be honourable, disciplined and noble; now it
> wants its owner to have public gratification . . . [It] has
> changed its demands from requiring us to be good to
> requiring us to be famous . . .[1]

This is a picture of adulthood gone AWOL. Adulthood probably looks now more like a holiday than at any other time in
the modern period, because so much of the work of adulthood
is only half done. Younger people have been getting the
wrong idea about adulthood for some time, and many of
them are now envious of the wrong things: fame, notoriety,
easy money. The many manuals out now that rhapsodize
fatherhood, for example, are written without the shadow of
the father much present in them. They tend to idealize the

father because their authors (and the culture itself) long for an ideal father. Those good ideas and helpful suggestions are a distortion of a genuine and clear longing for a living example of good endurance, which is so much more than just not making mistakes. They express a longing for the elder who has gone missing in action. It is a distortion so subtle and undetected that the elder longing is subverted into a yearning after celebrity, into the pursuit of being noticed, by anyone.

• • •

Those who have had the ashen experience in childhood of a parent dying or leaving for good know this common pattern in their own way. The agony that ensues in the child is unbearable, in large part because it comes from the absence of the longed-for parent, an absence which the child is powerless to redress or compensate for. The missing parent leaves a hole the shape of a mother or a father in the soul of the child. In a lunge toward sanity, the child shifts the location of the grief to make it manageable. The grief then comes not from the *absence* of the parent, not from outside, but from the *longing* for the absent parent, *from one's own longing*, inside. In other words, the grief is brought inside the soul's house, and personalized. The real problem, at last, is inside the self. The last stage, the one that makes everything bearable in the short run, where the missing parent can't intrude, the stage that brings almost irrevocable loss in the long run, is this: the desire and its grief are disowned, sent away for good — thrown out the window when no one is looking or buried beneath the basement stairs, they are forgotten and never found. The young man disowns his missing father and declares: I don't want him, whoever he is. I never had a car, and I never had a father. It's the same kind of feeling. Never had one, never needed one. Never missed one, never wanted one. Whatever.

Later, when the young man grows and marries, and the intimacy becomes grim and some kind of serious hardship is at the door, the desire for what has gone missing has a tremendous influence on how he handles hurt, betrayal, jealousy, and the like. When, as a teenager, you lose contact with your longing in this way, adulthood hasn't got much attraction to you. You sneer at it. You didn't ask to be born. You hang out only with people your own age, in malls. Getting older, you play fast and loose with the rules. Maybe you take some government money you don't need and won't pay back, just because you qualify. You are non-aligned, not attached to much, and you float. You don't join in, you don't work in and for the community. Your debts are only to yourself and your own. Your greatest fear in life is getting pooched in a business deal. No ashes, no grief, no gravity. No desire in the soul for the things that can sustain you. Later still, this misplaced desire comes forward in the form of disgust.

One afternoon, disgusted, bravo, you fall asleep.
You see yourself in a ballroom, your passions seated
before you in evening dress, swallow tails, bustles,
opera glasses, pearls.
You walk to the podium, turn to the orchestra

and conduct the overture to the master opera of neglect.
Purity of heart — wow!
Sounds performing without net erasing into wilderness of air.
Melodious, rambling rottings-away of bright edifices.
Desire gone to the drug store and never seen again.[2]

This poem by Canadian poet Tim Lilburn evokes the nausea so well. He describes the domestication and gutting of passion, and he places the responsibility for it squarely upon the one who has abdicated the business of growing down into his or her own life. "Neglect" describes it perfectly. Those so afflicted say, Nothing endures, and everything I do evaporates or rots. Purity of heart is a joke. I feel drugged by my loss of desire, and by forgetting what I miss, and by not asking again what I am here for. When you see me, pass by; I am a dangerous person. I am a disembodied spirit.

Well, all of this is a recipe for tremendous problems — including strife between generations, which is what we have now. Many will remember the much-proclaimed warning of a generation ago that no one over thirty should be trusted. The over-thirty types had been co-opted and corrupted by the system, so the party line went. They hadn't rebelled thoroughly, and they were too much from the Old Order. The Aquarians avoided the world of their parents because this thing about being co-opted by the system was contagious. Fears about the ease with which one can be corrupted crept into every relationship with someone older. One of the reasons the counterculture bred so rapidly was the fear that too much contact with the Establishment could dull one's mind or enslave one's soul. Typically, there were no elders in counterculture life, because experience was not to be trusted, because experience was the corrupter. The elders were the problem. They were irredeemable and just didn't get it, and to trust them would be to invite the enemy in. Better to cut them off at the knees, shorten the shelf life of their potent years, and make more room for the unsullied new guys. You could be infected by any errant trust of your elders.

A few years ago I was walking through Greenwich Village in New York City. It was a late spring afternoon and there was a predictable traffic jam on the narrow street. An older man in an upscale car, temporarily at the end of his patience and no doubt feeling some impotence in the situation, leaned on his horn for several seconds and howled something unintelligible out his window. It was an utterly useless gesture, given the gridlock ahead, but I guess it is common enough. A few younger men were sitting at a table outside a café across from him. One fellow, himself in a business suit and judging by his appearance not down on his luck, looked up at this aural intrusion into his day and, sneering at the older man, bellowed, "Yeah, yeah, yeah. Go make *money*." The contempt that was wrapped around the last word turned the phrase into a kind of curse. I remember how aggressive that curse was, and how unexpected. The younger guy, wearing the casually tailored armour of the young captain of e-business he probably was, howling his barely disguised envy and disgust at the older man, was Defender of the Faith of a Boomer youth no longer young.

I've begun to wonder whether there's not a more emphatic and troubled web connecting money and masculinity in the Boomer generation in particular. Could that be so? The older generation now in semi-retirement has had more experience with money and has perhaps worked out these queasy moral and ethical issues — or maybe that experience has just worn the old guys out and made them flaccid and unable to struggle any longer. And perhaps those under thirty-five or so have a simpler problem with money: they don't have much of it, and bleak prospects of having much of their own, ever. It's likely that they'd appreciate a crack at ethical ambivalence where money is concerned. Their anger and their envy over the resources and the attention devoted to the Boomer Bulge is regular fare in magazines and newspaper opinion columns. But so far, aside from the dot com millionaires, there's no deal for them.

For the Boomers, the struggle comes down to a war between the tyranny of a half-born, elderless maturity and the demands of a monied, mortgaged existence. The Boomers, on the cusp of being elders themselves, are struggling with the slowly dawning realization that half-lived measures are not working and that dismissing the elders leaves you very alone.

I was born during the night sea-journey . . .
I love the snow; I need privacy as I move.
I am all alone; floating in the cooking pot
on the sea, through the night I am alone.

I call out my wateriness in magnificent words.
That is the water man, but what of the land man?
He lives in a half-fixed house, with plank floor,
where things are half-said, half-sung, half-danced.
Constantly sieged by a power that can't get in,
I feed a multitude of cackling men, who beat
with sticks on the log walls. And when they are drunk
they fight over water, and spill it on the plank floor.[3]
— ROBERT BLY, "DECEMBER 23, 1926"

Here, Robert Bly might be describing an old struggle with his own masculinity and with older men, but it has the authentic sound of stilt-balanced self-doubt and self-loathing that I have heard from many men. That part of him which he calls "the land man" is crippled by a half-lived life and haunted by the rumour that it could — but won't — be some other way. The land man is clever and wordy but unhelped, elderless, private, and alone, and so the other men inside and outside him seem dangerous and primitive, which is a good description of how men often experience each other.

During the past two decades the inevitable movement of the Boomer generation into family making and careerism has occurred. There is often no elder to go to for advice, yet there is a serious need for help when it comes to the naïveté-induced ambivalence which the issues of money generate. That famous comic strip haiku comes to mind: We have met the enemy, and he is us. There is a kind of dependence-driven apathy when it comes to money. It also takes the form of being vulnerable to those who con and take. So we have in this generation perhaps an inordinate number of large-scale stock market scammers and con artists who operated loosely within the guidelines, who got caught, who blinked their corrupted innocence (that is, their naïveté) into the cameras. And those guidelines may have been a bit hazy, specifically because they reflected the ambivalence of those who were there to enforce them. In this generation there are high numbers of predators and prey, and they find each other.

The greed which has been blamed for much of the financial mayhem of the last two recessions, particularly in the real estate market, is a grasping born of this same corrupted "innocence." People with no experience in business were flipping their houses every six months, and people with no income were taking on mortgages they couldn't manage because it was either now or never. There were many beneficiaries who took without asking questions, and many victims who shrugged and signed and paid without asking questions. When you ask questions, you allow a bit more room for complicity or a (perhaps unwitting) acknowledgement of complicity.

There is in the Boomer generation a kind of naïveté that rages and fulminates and is sprayed indiscriminately, that rails at maturity, at moving to the next stage in life, at leaving the Garden. It claims and demands for itself a permanently divested life, free of compromise and entanglement, like The Little Prince — free of paralyzing ambivalence and confounding dependence on elders. This same generation that howled the Primal Scream now champions the Inner Child. I can only imagine what either of those rants might sound like to another generation. Both are strong metaphors for regression, and they both betray a nausea in the face of adult life, and in the face of spiritual life.

• • •

These ambivalences and entanglements, the compromises and dependencies, can all be found in attitudes about money. Years ago, the Boomers fired their parents and their elders, which didn't leave many heroes or living treasures standing. If you reject Mom and Dad and all they stand for in order to make your own world and your own truths, you have to reject their money, too, and their money habits, and their money pre-occupations and their money decisions and their money values.

Here is a true story that bundles together these themes of protracted adolescence and money nausea with gruesome, authentic clarity.

In April, 1992, a young man from a well-to-do East Coast family hitchhiked to Alaska and walked alone into the wilderness north of Mt. McKinley. Four months later his decomposed body was found by a party of moose hunters.[4]

So begins — and ends — the sad and bizarre story of twenty-two-year-old Christopher McCandless. Shortly after graduating university in the U.S., McCandless dropped off the face of his known world, the one he had been born into. He wandered across much of southwestern America, seeking with greater and greater success and severity to live without resorting to the paraphernalia of contemporary urban life: car, status, insurance, gnarled family relationships — and money. Referring to himself in the third person, McCandless wrote in his diary that during his wanderings, his quest to divest himself of the world had "taken a toll on his body. Over 25 pounds lost. But his spirit is soaring." Initially, it looks like a great story of a young man seeking his own voice, his own way. It looks noble, if extreme, and its apparent simplicity and purity of heart might seem even enviable. In fact, however, it shows how McCandless soared away from this world. Within a few years, he starved to death in Alaska in mid-summer in an abandoned bus, utterly unknown and alone.

McCandless's biographer, Jon Krakauer, tries to make sense of his subject's harsh choices. A neighbour told him that "Chris's parents were no different, really, than . . . anyone's parents. I think he would have been unhappy with any parents; he had trouble with the whole *idea* of parents."[5] He had a difficult relationship with his father in particular. Krakauer found himself identifying with McCandless in at least this one significant detail, as many men of his and my generation would: "I believe we were similarly affected by the skewed relationships we had with our fathers. And I suspect we had a . . . similar agitation of the soul."[6] As he grew up,

> Chris's resentment of his parents hardened, his sense of outrage over injustice in the world at large grew. [He] started

complaining about all the rich kids at Emory. More and more of the classes he took addressed such pressing social issues as racism and world hunger and inequities in the distribution of wealth. But despite his aversion to money and conspicuous consumption, Chris's political leanings could not be described as liberal . . . he was a vocal admirer of Ronald Reagan.[7]

In interviewing the young man's parents, Krakauer noted this:

Perhaps the greatest paradox concerned his feelings about money. [McCandless] . . . believed that wealth was shameful, corrupting, inherently evil — which was ironic because Chris was a natural-born capitalist with an uncanny knack for making a buck.[8]

Chris's sister observed that when he was younger he had "made a pile of money. He didn't seem interested in the money so much as the fact that he was good at making it. It was like a game, and the money was a way of keeping score."[9]

Chris McCandless was a lost boy. His distaste for the world, for adulthood, for the encumbrances of emotional connectedness with others constellated in his intense aversion to money. This is what makes his story more than just death by misadventure. He was, clearly, not indifferent to money. He hated it and everything he took it to mean. Money was connected to the world of his father, and McCandless was clearly disowning his father when he disowned his own and everyone else's money. And it cost him his life. Most men who disown their fathers do so with greater subtlety, and their deaths are more subtle and protracted as a result.

There is a shadowy little fantasy that is often played out in the generations that have lost their elders and their way. People suspect that to make moderate amounts of money, someone has to covet money and be forever concerned with the getting and the keeping of it. People scorn such a preoccupation with money. It is a sign of middling-hood, meagreness, juvenility. It is the sign of an amateur. It is a sign of people who lived through the Depression and were deformed by it. To make wads, though, the trick is to not care about money at all. To be an outrageous financial success, one must be blithe. One must not depend on it, not think about it, not count it, not want it. You hardly know it's there. Disengagement has often been imagined as the secret to absurd success. This is a common kind of scheming, and I've heard variations of it many times in my office. Buddhism has been very loosely embraced by some in the Boomer generation as an alternative to traditional Western religious belief. Mistakenly, Buddhism is thought to elevate this disengagement and aversion to the level of a spiritual practice, the practice of holding the world at a great distance, the practice of being unattached. This generation in its projections and fantasies about money has managed to have it both ways: the key to being both rich and clean is to be unconcerned with money. It is dread disguised as contemplation and as play. It is a dread of the world of the elders, a dread of adulthood, a dread of filth, a refusal to leave the Garden.

• • •

Many of those who make serious money and have written about it have embraced the making of money as a by-product of *playing the game of making money*. *Homo Ludens*: the anthropologists say that man is a game-playing being. Players are true believers of a kind. Play requires the more or less willing suspension of disbelief, or at least of suspicion. You may enter the game knowing that it is just a game, but the game requires the spirit of play and a full embrace of the reality of the game at hand. And the game has the power to conjure this full embrace. Just by playing, we bring this spirit of play into being. We know this from even casual sports encounters. The game carries us along until someone gets hurt or angry, or until someone quits out of boredom or disgust. When this happens, we feel that the spirit of play has left us and gone elsewhere. Everyone at once feels dispirited, abandoned, deflated, and defeated by the demise of the game, but the real cause is the collapse and flight of the spirit of play. Writers whose work is found in the "Business Leadership" section of the bookstore often see money making in this way, as a game — or a war game.

Dostoevsky the writer was also Dostoevsky the inveterate gambler. And he was gifted with insight into his own shadowy association with money, and his entanglement and fascination with hitting it big without working. He wrote that his chief pleasure was playing the game of making money from nothing. "The main thing is the play itself. I swear that greed for money had nothing to do with it, though heaven knows I am sorely in need of it."[10] He makes his gambling sound like a pure, innocent, childlike pursuit, and you can hear this aversion to being touched by the grime of a preoccupation with money. It may have been for Dostoevsky that this was an aesthetic thing, a question almost of hygiene. You can also hear this faith in the spirit of play. Dostoevsky was a true believer, though an unsuccessful player as a gambler, and it cost him dearly.

Thinking later on his subsequent time in jail, Dostoevsky had a wider and more discerning insight into money:

Money is coined liberty, and so it is ten times dearer to the man who is deprived of freedom. If money is jingling in his pocket, he is half consoled, even though he cannot spend it. But money can always and everywhere be spent . . . Even vodka could be got in prison. Pipes were strictly forbidden, but every one smoked them. Money and tobacco saved them from scurvy and other diseases. Work saved them from crime; without work the convicts would have devoured one another like spiders in a glass jar. In spite of this, both work and money were forbidden.[11]

So he had learned a few things about money in the interim — that it was more than a game — and he was willing to give money its due.

The poet John Keats admitted to a similar loathing for the indelicacy of dealing with money. In a letter to a friend, he lamented having to endure the bottomless and eternal misery of a visit to his bank.

> I shall have a little trouble in procuring the Money and a great ordeal to go through — no trouble indeed to anyone else — or ordeal either. I mean I shall have to go to town some thrice, and stand in the Bank an hour or two — to me worse than anything in Dante.[12]

Artists are an interesting lot where money and maturity are concerned. Dostoevsky and Keats were both marvellously gifted artists, but their confessions about money more than hint at a regressed inability to discern and cope. I, alas, recognize my own bank anxiety in Keats' hellish loathing of the experience. And I recall from my own vain attempt to succeed in the business of art that for some artists, it is a badge of honour to be miserably dependent on a dealer or an agent to make deals for them. These middlemen are cursed regularly as Pharisees and bloodsuckers, but all the while the artists swear off learning about their own money. It is a largely unspoken article of faith among some artists that money interferes with art making, and even that the spirit of money is hostile to the spirit of art making.

The painter Salvador Dali was an alchemist in many respects. In a declaration that would have been at home in any alchemical manual of the Middle Ages, Dali said: the moment base matter turns to gold — that's how you spiritualize matter. There is the hint Dali gives: matter *needs* to be spiritualized. Alchemy is unthinkable and unnecessary if the world, or matter, is seen to have a soul which your soul has kinship with. Dali's estate, as it happened, was bedevilled by this very enterprise. Toward the end of his days, Dali was found to have signed reams of empty sheets of paper, which later were sold adorned with prints of dubious quality and provenance. The subsequent devaluation was not restricted to these particular blank cheques; the monetary value of much of Dali's later work suffered in the marketplace for this dabble with alchemy. While it is always a riotous encounter when calling up the spirits of money, you do not necessarily get gold for your trouble. Signing your name on empty sheets of paper for money can draw your name itself down into the void.

I remember reading an interview with Picasso, who was the dark king of money and art in the twentieth century. Well into his sixties, he presented a ribald and essentially *puer,* or adolescent, sensibility, and he not coincidentally made an unimaginable killing during his lifetime. Picasso did not feign disinterest in or disgust with the art market. When the discussion turned to why he was so successful in the marketplace, he did not talk about his art. He said, "I am the beneficiary of other people's greed." Picasso was truly fascinated by the art market, and he traded on his fame constantly. I read once that he went so far as to write cheques for considerable sums as a cunning way of saving money, since he knew that they would never be cashed. His signature was worth more to the payee than the amount on the cheque.

Picasso's art, though not unanimously embraced, had sub-stance. There are hosts of artists today who achieve more notoriety than Picasso did, and not because their art is better. It is because — such is our time — they are famous for being famous. The art world, like the Inner Judge that Bly wrote about, has changed. It no longer wants artists to be good; it wants them to be famous.

• • •

For the past half-dozen years I've been running a program of grief work for men who have lost a loved one. Though ostensibly about grief and loss, the program is equally con-cerned with understanding mature masculinity. A few years ago, a young man was referred to me so I could help him with his grief over the death of his brother. He said he might have attended the program if there'd been women in the group, but he was not coming otherwise. I asked him why. Well, his father had abandoned the family years before, and he'd grown used to the absence of a man, and he didn't need to be near men now. In fact, though he didn't say so, his distaste told me he hated the idea. There was no real choosing for this man, no matter how he explained it to himself. The fact is that he couldn't have handled being in the same room with a half-dozen older men. He was the land man of Bly's poem, and other men were savage and untrustworthy to him. Ironically, the father hunger that would have stirred in him would have been something overwhelming and, instinctively, he knew it.

As men of his ilk will do, he turned down the invitation to be initiated into the world of fathers, titans, and dangerous characters, and I didn't hear from him again.

The work this men's group undertakes weekly has taught me tremendous lessons about masculinity and money. One story immediately comes to mind. Jim (not his real name) freely admitted when he joined that he did not trust men and was ill at ease in a group of us. To his credit, he stayed with the group and became a valued presence for the others and for me. Jim's wife had died just prior to his joining up, and it was only months later that her will was finally being dealt with. The will provided him with her full estate, which was considerable, and essentially left out her adult children from another marriage. Jim had not attended too much to money issues during his marriage, and he was surprised and a little perturbed by this development. For the first time, he would have to chain himself to the money wheel. While, amidst the gnashing of teeth, Jim was debating what he would gift to each of his deceased wife's children, it emerged that a clerical error in the filing of the will had cast its authority and directions very much in doubt. The children subsequently obtained lawyers and disputed the will. Jim felt savaged and violated by their attacks — particularly by their suspicion that he had engineered their exclusion from the will.

Because he was searingly honest with himself in our presence, Jim came to admit that his wife's money — and it had been substantially her money — had insulated him from many of the usual fears and insecurities a family's provider experiences, and subsequently from the growing into personhood which such struggles can initiate. Once she was gone, he experienced her children's attack as the attack of siblings. He was disabled and paralyzed by their envy and their accusations. His wife's money had bought him comfort — but not substance — and a frail kind of security that could bear no challenge and no scrutiny. He had known this about himself all along. But it was in the process of contending with lawyers and bankers and hostile stepchildren that he began to grow that substance in himself. His wife's money had sustained his childhood well into his middle age years, and his wife's money was now giving him the chance to become a person. It was no coincidence that a man with these kinds of self-doubts also found men threatening and unsympathetic, and no coincidence that money figured both in his self-absorption and in his becoming a person.

I write this in the middle of the season of tax calculation and retirement fund contributions, as we are being subjected to another round of advertisements selling all kinds of financial planning services. There is one radio ad that displays the regressed dread of money so painfully well. A young boy asks his father if he can talk to him about his allowance. Being the accommodating and attentive sort of father most fathers would like to be, Dad encourages him to go ahead. The boy wonders whether he should invest his allowance in long-term bonds with a certain income or short-term instruments carrying risk and high return, or . . . The acronyms are just flying. The father stutters and mumbles and tries to cover himself by directing

113

the boy's attention to a video game.

The father seems to be a thirty- or forty-something man, and the ad appeals to his secret fear and certainty that everybody understands money but him. The ad exposes his self-loathing in these matters, and then offers an investment advisor to help him cope with it. The ad was no doubt put together with research and focus groups, and the ad agency no doubt is aware of the theme we're discussing here, and especially how it flares up at investment deadlines and tax preparation time. It is a shaming advertisement and a grotesque piece of psychological moralizing. It says: The only way you can keep up with your own children is with our help. It is okay to hate yourself, as long as you bring in the experts. The expert investment advisor is the surrogate father and the better father for this boy. It is simply a question of who has a larger penis. The guys who know about money, this ad says, *including the boy*, are the better endowed.

• • •

I grew up through the latter half of the 1950s and into the sixties without a father. Younger people may not realize that fatherless homes were not nearly as common then as they are now. A fatherless house in the late 1950s really was a blighted place, and a place of considerable frailty. In school, my sister and I were treated as though a case of the plague had broken out in our home. The stigmatization was subtle, and it was presented as compassionate concern. I remember a very distinct feeling after my father left that the house itself was vulnerable and suddenly insubstantial, that the walls were not as strong as they'd been before, that the roof couldn't hold up, and that it wouldn't take much to devastate the place. Many of those feelings came from the fears aroused by our uncertain financial status and our sense that no one would save us. In a situation like that, a father and his money are as consequential by virtue of their absence as a mother and her attempts to provide are by virtue of their presence.

This association of a father's absence from the home with deep feelings of insecurity hovers in the current conviction that separated fathers must pay to see their children. (This, in spite of the fact that legal safeguards exist in most jurisdictions to deal with the issue.) It is not uncommon in those situations for a mother to withhold access in the event that the father is in support arrears. But it is equally common to find fathers who withhold support because the mothers have found new partners or because they believe the mothers are interfering in their relationship with their children to the point where the children do not want to see them. This is not to spread blame around — there is usually more than enough — but only to show how both genders tend to accept this connection between money and paternity without acknowledging that they do so and without thinking through their feelings about that connection. Unexamined, this connection is the source of much of the heartache that accompanies separation and divorce.

It's extremely important that fathers take the relationship between paternity and money seriously. The world around them surely does. My clients have taught me that men who have not worked on their fears and confusions over money struggle with fatherhood. Whether we agree or not, fatherhood in contemporary North American culture is not accorded as great a sense of inviolability, inevitability, or naturalness as motherhood. My work in the family court system has shown me that motherhood tends to be understood as a given which commences at the birth of a child and endures come what may. Fatherhood, on the other hand, is not automatically established by the birth of the child. Instead, it is established by the decisions made and the actions taken throughout the child's infancy and childhood and well into adolescence. A father is, in other words, as a father does. That's what the new brother-in-law was telling the groom.

• • •

By now it is becoming clear that money should not be blamed for our behaviour around it, and that we should not equate projection with ethical irresponsibility or shadow with evil. To blame money for our confusion over it is the same impulse as to blame your child for the anger that you feel toward him or her. Of course, this is so common as to usually pass without notice or comment, but this very confusion and silence has helped to isolate money from the life of the spirit. The demonizing of money is an *expression* of this confusion, not the resolution of it.

A good antidote for the dilemmas outlined here might be to go to a self-directed financial planning seminar. A person might get some guidance there about where their money should go. But I am always wary when it comes to professional money handlers making it their job to arouse my anxieties in order to reassure me and make work for themselves. The program there tends to be to sell my anxiety back to me tarted up as responsible thinking. I think a better move would be to cultivate relationships with older people. Specifically, younger men and older men need each other. If they hang around each other long enough, they each find what the other's life has to teach. The older men need not be exemplary people. A younger man is not at the older man's side to learn only the right way or how to avoid making mistakes. He is there to learn how to learn. Mentors are better in the long run than experts. The problems in this generation are not primarily about money, no matter what kind of financial mayhem we may experience. But looking at money helps men see that many of the problems they encounter are ones of mistrust of experience and age.

Some years ago I tried to make a go of it as a professional sculptor. With no guidance and no education, I tried to make a living at it. After some disastrous experiences in the marketplace, coming from a lethal combination of naïve trust and betrayal, I sought out a sculptor, an older man, who was still continuing to work and sell. I was a great admirer of his endurance and his fortitude. I was also much too envious, I now realize, of his set-up — of how customers would come to him looking for work to buy. It looked so easy.

We sat in his backyard, overlooking a terrific garden of his own design, including sculptures, carp pools, and cypress trees. He was still strong and still flint-eyed, though there may have been a little loneliness around him. His marriage hadn't gone particularly well, and he'd lived a long time in the house with boarders instead of family. I was trying to steer the conversation around so he could tell me about his canniness and success, so he could give me some clue and maybe get me into the inner circle of privilege. Maybe I could make of a go of things, with his help and blessing. Maybe, I admit to myself now, I could benefit from his connections and hitch a ride on his success. He more or less ignored me, and after some silence said this:

> I've been pretty fortunate. I stayed healthy. My wife didn't turn my kids against me. I've stayed busy doing what I love to do.
> I have enough money, the house is paid for, and I don't need much else. I got everything I asked for.
> But I never asked for love.
> And I never got it.

It was a lesson about adolescent envy he taught me, and a lesson about the strong demands and steep cost that are to be paid in the struggle toward being a whole human being. That meeting in his garden gave by taking. It took the false nobility of my motivation for being there, and it gave one living example of a man trying to make his peace with his life.

Money, Sex, Betrayal

Where exactly is the money complex hidden?
Most often it hides in the guises of love,
where so much soul is anyways hidden.[1]
— JAMES HILLMAN

There's a saying in the therapy business, which, loosely translated, goes like this: By their sex and their money you will know them. It's a bit coarse and blithe, but it has earned its keep as an assessment tool. Whatever problems people bring to counselling, the counsellor is best served by sooner or later asking them about their sex lives and their money lives — how in both instances they "do it." This doesn't mean that these are the only two areas where problems show themselves. But it does mean that if people have communication problems, they will have problems talking about sex and money. If they have intimacy fears, they will have some fearfulness about the implicating power and the healing power of sex and money. If they are shamed in one, shame in the other is not far away.

When things become difficult in intimate relationships, the apparent estrangement between sex and money falls away, and to our considerable horror we discover their kinship, right in our own house. This is plainly seen in households where the main money earner loses a job. In families where men become unemployed, one of the first discernible casualties is in their sexual life. There is very often an experience of impotence, with all of the shaming it brings, and impotent rage, when the man loses his way of providing for his family. This instinct toward impotence affects more than the man. Women in therapy report a dramatic decrease in their sexual attraction to their unemployed husbands, which completes the circle. These homes are flat and arid places.

The connection between sex and money in the confounding of intimacy may not be clear, either to those beset by unemployment or to their families and neighbours, but it is dramatic and unmistakeable. "I never had so many cases of impotency [sic], for instance, as when the stock market fell — not only stock brokers, but people in general."[2] That was the informed observation of Xaviera Hollander, otherwise known to posterity as The Happy Hooker. Though the sagacity of her take on things may be suspect, and her reference to her tricks as "cases" may be nervy or unseemly to mental health professionals, the sheer scope of her experience lends merit to her sentiments on the subject.

There is a point in our dealings with money and sex where, usually under duress, we become very much ourselves, where we confess ourselves. One way of accounting for this would be to say that it is in the nature of money and sex that they oblige us to be ourselves, in spite of our preferred inclination to the contrary. The promises and vows and good intentions fall away, and the deal we have struck with ourselves and our partners begins to make its presence known and starts to take effect.

Money and sex are liquid in their form and their meaning, as we've noticed. Sometimes they spell domination. Other times they come in the form of supplication. We have to give them shape, a definition of limits, a context, to coax a function and a meaning out of them. We are discernible in the shape of sex and money, in the form that they take in our personal and cultural lives. We experience as immutable those meanings which sex and money have for us, as if they were well established, clear to all, self-evident, and enduring — though none of this is true. They are grails we inadvertently fill with our own longing. And they are strips of litmus paper. Both sex and money are chaotic when there is no container of social convention to tame them and force them into simple meaning and function. These attempts to tame them are entirely doomed, of course, because sex and money will always threaten to overflow their banks and change their course and their meaning. They will not stay put. They bring dishevelment and anxiety, and they are distinctly undomesticated. So the meanings and significances we give them — however mild or wild they may seem — are attempts to rein in the chaos and bring crazy money and crazy sex quietly into the house, trying in vain to leave the furniture where it is and the walls intact.

• • •

The fact that much of our culture is at pains to keep sex and money distinct and at a distance attests to our subliminal suspicions and misgivings about their volatility and their liquidity. One at a time is hard enough to manage. Both together is asking for trouble. The places where they meet, and the consequences of their proximity — in prostitution and in marriage, to take the obvious examples — are deep in the shadows. Consider the kind of language used to describe the experience of one person getting the better of another in a business deal, be it shady or legitimate: the verbs are identical to those describing various sexual acts, and few of them are genteel or considerate of anyone's sensibilities. Business partners see themselves getting into bed with each other, and they bargain for a certain outcome. Some kind of violation usually ensues.

Over the years, I have presided at the dissolution of too many marriages in my office. These moments bring a tremendous amount of suffering to all, regardless of whose idea it was to split. Later on, after the visit to the lawyers, the bravely begun but doomed marital enterprise is reduced to sniping, posturing, and motions for sole custody. What many find most monstrous is that the dénouement of a marriage is principally an exercise in accounting. It does all come down to money, without doubt. The redistribution of money is the last rite of the marriage. And the state intervenes twice. First, it obliges naïve people to make reckless and groundless promises at the wedding ceremony. Then at the end, it says, "All right. You will make some material sacrifice here. Your long-term sexual arrangement, the one you thought you got for nothing, now has to be paid for." If you are doubtful that this is the line drawn by the state, bear this in mind: in most jurisdictions, the legal date of separation, which marks the end of goodwill and the end of the voluntary distribution of the marriage's assets, is the last time the couple slept together or had sex. In the eyes of the law, the end of sex in marriage is the beginning of accounting.

It is not a recent tendency to wonder about and shudder at the kinship between sex and money. Here is an offhand piece of anthropology from the Greek historian Herodotus, who lived from about 480 to about 425 BCE.

> The customs of the Lydians differ little from those of the
> Grecians, except that they prostitute their females. They are
> the first of all nations we know of that introduced the art of
> coining gold and silver; and they were the first retailers.[3]

It is difficult to tell here whether Herodotus is admiring, describing, or condemning his neighbours the Lydians. Evidently, he found their entrepreneurial spirit in all matters noteworthy. The art of coining would have been a leap into abstraction, as it transformed currency from real value to symbolic value. Herodotus seems to have found that the

Lydians' innovative spirit in this area paralleled their prostituting practices. The coincidence certainly captured his attention.

Closer to home in time and space, Samuel Butler, writing at the dawn of the last century in England, noticed that

> *next to sexual matters* there are none upon which there is such complete reserve between parents and children as on those connected with money. The father keeps his affairs as closely as he can to himself and is most jealous of letting his children into a knowledge of how he manages his money. *His children are like monks in a monastery as regards money.* Nevertheless he thinks himself ill-used if his son, on entering life, falls a victim to designing persons whose knowledge of how money is made and lost is greater than his own [italics mine].[4]

Butler sees obvious links between money, sex, and religious imagery — a more common connection than is expected or tolerated in Western culture. His words invoke the "purity" or "virginity" of the spiritually inclined mind in the matter of money, something we will question presently. They hint at the terminal naïveté that such a father breeds in his son when he fails to tutor him in matters concerning money. Because of his ill-conceived efforts to shelter the young boy, both father and son are financial and sexual prudes. Such a father would shudder as much at the prospect of his young son finding his bank book in his jacket pocket as he would if his son should find a "men's magazine" in a box in the basement. He has set up his son for naïveté, betrayal, and humiliation in the marketplace and in any future marriage by not sharing his knowledge, experience, failures, or misgivings with him. Butler also registers the same connection as Herodotus; there is a kinship, however unclear or unsanctioned, between sex and money.

If you are skeptical about the overtones of this account and if you do not recognize this pattern of puritanism and fascination that surrounds money concerns in family life, consider these questions:

1. Do you and your partner have separate or joint bank accounts, or both? Why? Has that arrangement always been as it is now, and how did it come about? Are you content to let it stand, or do you feel comfortable wanting to change it? How would you go about changing it?

2. Do you know how much money your partner has? Does s/he know how much you have? Why? Do you know how much money your in-laws have, and the disposition of your partner in their wills?

3. Do your children know how much money you have? How much you make? How did they find out, if they did, and if not, why do they not know?

4. Have you had The Sex Talk with your children? Have you had The Money Talk with your children? What did you tell them? What did they ask you?

Aversion is avowal in human affairs. Whether we are gimpy or aggressive in our intimate relationships when it comes to money, we can read anxiety there. It is one of the covert articles of Protestant faith (of which I am a product) that money confounds intimacy utterly, and this prejudice has been shared with the larger culture. When I showed an early version of these ideas to an investment advisor, he responded by saying, "You're right. Money's terrible for relationships. Nothing worthwhile comes from it." It was interesting to me how, as he started thinking about money in life, he became uneasy and aversive, even though money was his area of expertise. It seemed that his familiarity with the ways of money only deepened his mistrust of it.

• • •

Many people in marriage or other intimate relationships grapple with this by assigning the murky money-handling function to only one partner. Early on, in a fit of rationalist decision making, one partner will suggest that Efficiency is a good organizing principle for domestic life. Everyone should do what they do best! I'm good with numbers! Let me handle the money!

Of course, that sounds as if it makes good sense — using each other's strengths to each other's benefit. If it's your partner who is perplexed when investment deadlines and tax time come around, you might think it's a bit pathetic, but also kind of cute. And your partner's willingness to let you do the thinking for both of you when it comes to money is one of the

things you like about them. It seems reasonable and support-
ive, and it shows good judgement on their part. You go along
with it. This is the kind of seduction that lurks in another
trust company ad that I've heard at investment deadline time.
Its tag line is, "You do the living. We'll do the math" — as
if you can't do both. This is a sad separation in thinking and
living, but a common one.

What happens next? The one who disowns the money functions remains shy, skittish, awkward, and underdeveloped in
that area. Seven years later, they know no more about money
than they ever did. And maybe they know less. Everyone
assumes that because no one has raised a fuss, this arrangement is agreeable and will stand indefinitely. Everyone
assumes that it is working. This ignorance isn't neutral, however, and it's not inert. It breeds dependence, anxiety, and
resentment. The one who begged off fretting over the family
finances will often later blame money — the lack of it or the
faulty distribution of it — for some of the family problems. And
eventually, that person blames the one handling the money for
the problems. That's just inevitable. This is what follows. The
underdeveloped one will sling a stone that sounds like this:
"You always kept me in the dark about our money." And the
one who has handled the money all this time, with no thanks,
will sling a stone of their own: "Well, it was never really *our*
money, now was it. When was it ever *our* money?"

It was jointly held in title, in the joint account or in law
perhaps, but certainly the spiritual and psychological interest
accruing to the *handling* of it did not circulate freely between

the "partners." It got stuck in the hands of one person. It would be a lie to call them partners at that point. The one who disowned the handling of money surrendered any legitimate claim to joint decision making, to being informed, to developing some security and some dexterity with money. By never handling, worrying about, or deciding about money, the "clean one" was never inoculated from the regressive tendencies that surface when anyone deals with money. Being informed is implicating: news about money woes drags a person into the fray of coping, worrying, and feeling vulnerable. The regressive part of us says, Better to stay away.

Another investment ad I've seen shows a picture of a little boy pulling a wagon. The text under him reads, "Remember when you didn't worry about money?" Regression, regression, regression: this is the financial industry's answer to money anxiety. "Abandon the field!" it preaches, "Let us do the work!" Interest rates, penalties, payment schedules, all of it is confounding stuff to children and to the one unfamiliar with the ways of money. The one who handled it got paid for that job by being abandoned to it, left alone with the filthy stuff, but also by developing some calluses and a familiarity, a facility, an intimacy with money — an intimacy that became monogamous, that excluded the partner. It's then a matter of time before the underdeveloped one calls down the C-word. They'll say, "You always wanted to control things! It always went the way *you* wanted it to!" When that disavowal finally comes reeling out of the shadows, it is snarling and salivating, and it wants someone to pay. The conviviality of the old arrangement, the gratitude that one partner may have felt — or the relief — when the other took over the money management, the cuteness and the innocence, the noble sentiments, the feeling of "us" — they are all long gone.

This "expertise" approach doesn't work well in intimacy — at least not for long. Think of what it's like when a person comes home from work into a domestic scene that is already underway. That person has a hard time for the first fifteen minutes. He or she has been on top of things (or has been trying to get there) all day, but at home, there is no room for that kind of skill. There is no top to get on top of. Being it, doing it, is what is called for. It is not a matter of holding off until you've got it right, then taking over. Intimacy wants workers, not bosses. You must learn about the things you avoid, you must practise them and embrace them. Share the anxieties about money and the work of handling money. *That is intimacy.*

Men have known for a long time, and women are finding out now, that the marketplace will reward you handsomely for "maximizing your potential," which is code for "sticking to what you are good at." But it warns that one should not wander off into those things that one does not know. Don't learn, unless your learning is an addendum to your expertise, done on your own time. You will otherwise be punished for displaying your incompetence, your naïveté, your amateur self. Oh, they say they want a well-rounded employee. But Efficiency demands first and foremost that you fit-the-hell-in. That can only happen if your expert self is working expertly.

This is a crazy kind of paradox I'm offering. I'm asking you to do the things that do not come easily to you. Abandon completely the idea that intimate relationships should "work" the way all your household machines should. Efficiency has no place in intimate life and soul life. Let your expertise take care of itself — which sounds not coincidentally like: Let the dead bury the dead. You should care for your aversions, your amateur self, the neglected part of you. Do what you are not good at. Visit the unvisited parts of yourself, regularly. Be awkward and unpolished and learning at home and when you are alone with yourself. That is your soul's work.

The Soul's Gold

God made everything out of nothing, but the
nothingness shows through.
— PAUL VALÉRY

These are darkening times, it would seem. The terrorism that has come to the United States, at the time I write this,
has reached deep into the young, grim, and isolated heart of
North American culture and brought out dread, numbness,
hysteria, and a taste for vengeance. The threats of more terrorism, and war, are palpable. The terrorism has many faces, and
it did not begin or end in New York or Afghanistan. It is a
crazy quilt spun from the insane rantings of monocultural,
monotheistic, soul-killing, tribalist ideologies, and many people
have wrapped themselves in that cloak. In my work I have
seen that these events and their immediate aftermath have
detonated a personal and almost cosmic grief that has

overwhelmed many, many people. Walking past newspaper box headlines you get flashcards of the apocalypse: War, Terror, Revenge — and Recession. In the early days after the attacks, the governments asked the people, of all things, to go to the malls. Shopping and spending are now part of North America's anti-terrorism campaign, and the temples of want are the battleground. One recent radio broadcast featured a woman saying, "Oh God, it was awful. I had a terrible dream. That bin Laden man was chasing me and he was after my money." Two professional men, in quiet tones, said, "Well, what happened was awful, of course, but if you have money and can afford to wait, this is a great time to invest." When those towers melted into ashes and dust, people began coming to an awareness that the grand edifice of corporate capitalism, which seemed so monolithic, so global, and so irresistible, was frail and impermanent in ways that few had suspected. So rational, so powerful, so adamant, so vulnerable. The frailty is a simple one: the whole shebang works only to the extent that we believe in it. How easy it was to rob Western consumers of their confidence.

These are times, as the American poet William Stafford warned, when

It is important that awake people be awake,
or a breaking line may discourage them back to sleep;

the signals we give — yes or no, or maybe —
should be clear: the darkness around us is deep.[1]

How is a person to come to the wakefulness that Stafford is pleading for, and how is a person to stay awake? So far in this book, we've looked at the trouble that money brings into relationships between cultures and between people. But money also has the power to darken and provoke a person's soul. It provokes the soul's desires, and it has a place in the soul's business. To discover something about these desires and where money belongs within them, clear language needs to be used. Well-spoken words are midwives to wakefulness.

• • •

First, why talk about soul at all? It is not so difficult to talk about money. It is possible to agree about what money is, to some degree, because it is not *that* intangible. The same, alas, cannot be said for the soul. There is precious little soul talk in the workplace, in the media, or in the schools. In fact, soul talk is discouraged in the schools, and in some jurisdictions it is outlawed altogether. The places where people meet and learn and work have little soul talk in them. At the same time, attendance at the old places which might have recognized and fed the hunger for soulfulness, the places of worship, are on the wane. For many, they are useless, destructive, or entirely extinct. How could an instinct for soulfulness survive this diminution and neglect?

Well, hunger is part rumour, an appetite for things not quite present, and part conviction, a faith that those things exist somewhere. An Italian woman I know has told me a bit of Mediterranean folk wisdom that her mother passed on to her while they cooked together: Food makes hunger. It is not the *absence* of food, which the logician in us would suppose, but the *presence* of food, that creates the desire, the hunger, the yearning. Her wisdom on this point can be experienced at any time. Fast for a while, and watch your attachment to food wither. I discovered that this was true many autumns ago when I was working in the Mediterranean on an old sailing ship which had been mauled by a gale and was dangerously low on food and water. We found in the first day or two without food that we fantasized constantly about what we'd eat when we were rescued. After that, the fantasies faded with the hunger, and food had no claim on us.

This wisdom can help us here. It is the *presence* of a thing that creates the hunger for it. It is the presence of the soul that makes the *desire* for soulfulness in this world. This longing is not nostalgia for things passed away. The hunger for the spiritual thing *is* a spiritual thing, and the work I do has consistently persuaded me that a hunger for soulfulness, however ill defined or misconstrued, is pervasive in our culture. This desire for the spiritual is to be *trusted* — trusted as a good indication of the gathering presence of the sacred at this hard and harrowed end of one millennium and the daunting, haunted beginning of another.

We have to do something about this idea of "my soul" or "your soul" and come to a finer and, I hope, useful distinction between *soul* and what I will call *self*. The self is to me an acquisition and an accomplishment, something that you, your parents, and your environment have wrought. It is like a series of accretions, borrowings, and inheritances, bound together by the necessity of having to be a consistent "someone" in the world. The self — its development and its frailties — is the preoccupation of psychology. When most people use the word "I," this is the self they are talking about, and this is the self who is usually doing the talking. The self proceeds as if all of life were subject to either its approval or its disapproval. When we talk about ourselves, a little imperialism often comes into our voice, as if we have cornered the market on what our life means, and on who or what we are. The self tends to swagger a bit and is usually dangerously low on humility when it talks. Of course, this does not do justice to the mountain of psychological writing that exists on this subject, but it will do as a thumbnail sketch.

The soul is a subtler and more poetic thing. It is more like an abiding presence than a tenacious accomplishment, and more a quality of approach than an identity. It is more a way than it is a thing. We might be better to speak of soulfulness.

Selling out the soul to the viewpoint of something more literal is not the answer to the problem of alleviating the soul's distress. There is a relief that comes not from simple answers and the courage of conviction, but from increased ambivalence, complexity and . . . the courage to criticise one's own convictions. This is the soul's way. It heals by differentiating problems, by mediating and making differences within them. [2]

135

Psychologist Greg Mogenson suggests that the soul's work is done by enduring contesting visions and claims, not by resolving them. Personal spiritual struggles with money need to be approached soulfully. I will take Mogenson's guidance in avoiding simple answers and resolutions. As we've observed from the beginning, money is magic, and a certain capacity for magical thinking of the kind British writer Dudley Young stands by is crucial to understanding what money does in one's life:

> The world's soul is composed of all those powers that seem to move invisibly and immaterially. Unlike us primitive man was not disposed to separate his own soul from the world-soul. This simply cannot be done: if you want to traffic with the invisible, you *have* to use magic. Because we have forgotten this . . . we are . . . more ignorant of [the soul's] desires than were our primitive forbears.[3]

The self is something we lay claim to. The soul is what lays claim to us. Soulfulness is not a human quality. It is a quality that human beings partake in, a quality that can be found in how you move, how you see things, how you talk and ponder and eat and love. Soulfulness is in the tea and rice of your life. It is a kind of language, and in its calm face we can recognize ourselves and each other, and we can see the way of the holy and the way the natural world has of being itself. The soul's way makes and sustains our kinship with the world and with strangers, and as we have seen, there is hell to pay when this kinship is forgotten. The world-soul contains and embraces and sustains all those things that humans find are implacable and opposite, and it gives humans a means of understanding how to live inside their contending ways. With this quality of soulfulness in our minds, we are now on the track of our soul's desires.

Many North American religious traditions seem to have tragic and revealing flaws in their teachings about money. The contemporary religious or spiritually inclined person tends to view money as inevitably hostile to the soul, and seductive. Those who traffic in money or who think about it too much are cursed without knowing it, they say, and the only good antidote is disinterest or, better still, hostility to money. The biblical claim that it is easier for a camel to pass through the needle's eye than for a rich man to enter the Kingdom of God is read precisely in this way, as we all know. It is a way of making sure that money stays in the shadows, where it belongs. Christians of a certain ilk, for example, continue to thrill at the prospect of the rich members of the congregation being castigated by the Jesus example, for giving only out of their abundance, for not "giving till it hurts."

The Christian Gospel stories include a scene that shows this is not a modern prejudice (Mark 12:41–44, Luke 21:1–4). Jesus is at the door of the temple treasury with his friends, and they are observing the giving of alms and offerings. The rich people are achieving considerable status with their substantial offerings, and into their midst comes a woman who leaves a paltry sum. The witnesses of this act probably showed consternation or indignation. At their most noble, those reactions may have come from a sense that God and the community had not been well served by the small offering. Jesus' answer was an invitation to consider that the rich man had given out of his abundance, while the woman had given out of her poverty. You tell me, he says, who gave more.

If this were a story laid out to pillory rich people, or to excoriate those overly involved with money, you'd expect to hear some condemnation of this kind of traffic. You'd expect to hear some exhortation to the same kind of disinterest or aloofness that now characterizes the Boomer's money conundrums. But money comes in for no criticism whatsoever in the story. The woman in the story is not elevated above the giving of money, *nor is God elevated above the receiving of it.* Jesus isn't pleased with her because she turned her back on the whole proposition of tithing and decided just to run with good intentions. *She also gave money.* If the presence of money was so diabolical in the life of the spirit, we'd have to say that she's not free from this particular devil, and we could expect Jesus to point her in the right direction, away from the stuff. We could expect him to say, "Look, don't you know money is the root of all evil?" But he doesn't do that. So money is not to blame — according to Jesus, at least. That is a spiritual truth, I would say.

The view expressed in this story is that money, being so quixotic, has certain powers that are not to be ignored. Chief among them might be the power to reveal all the misgivings, all the strivings, all the frailties and futilities which we bring to anything this awe-full. All this is hinted at when Jesus asks his listeners to look to where the money came from. He is saying, Never mind the bank or the strongbox or the pocket. The money comes from somewhere in you. Find where that is. When you find it, you'll find what you truly treasure, and hoard, and fear.

> *A certain ruler questioned him saying,*
> *"Good teacher, what shall I do to inherit eternal life?"*
> *He said to him,*
> *"One thing you still lack; sell all that you possess and*
> *distribute it to the poor . . ." But when he heard these things*
> *he became very sad for he was extremely rich.*
> *And Jesus . . . said,*
> *"How hard it is for those who are wealthy to enter the king-*
> *dom of God. For it is easier for a camel to go through the eye*
> *of a needle than for a rich man to enter the kingdom of God."*
> — LUKE 18:18, 22–25

This kind of teaching story is often used to pillory rich people, or people who have aspirations to wealth. It reads like a ready-made rationale for a hatred of money and rich men. Between Jesus, Luther, and Freud, there is nothing but to conclude, it seems, that money robs you of happiness in this life and keeps you out of heaven in the next.

Let me offer another way of hearing the story. What if it's not money that imprisons a rich person, nor only the attitudes that a rich person has about money? What if it's the attitudes and prejudices that *others* have about the rich man and his money, and the ways they treat him, that keep that man in misery and purgatory? If so, then the obligation to help the rich man find the Kingdom doesn't lie only with the rich man. That obligation is shared with his relatives and his neighbours. Their unexamined attitudes compromise the object of their scorn and ridicule just as surely as they condemn themselves. Old prejudices afflict more than those who inflict them on others.

The Jesus example is a familiar enough story, particularly among many North Americans, so it might be useful to pursue it a little further. The strain of reading the stories of his life is a good spiritual discipline, because it requires considerable effort to bear the human example in mind, and to recognize one's own struggles in that human example. Jesus' example is also a good one for our purposes because in it we see the struggles of a man striving to live out his spiritual calling and convictions — not in a monastic cell but in the world, in the circus of daily life. In particular, Jesus was obliged more than once to sort out the role of money in a spiritual life, and he had to articulate a place that money would occupy in the Kingdom which he envisioned in this world.

The story of the Three Temptations in the wilderness echoes a theme found in many of the world's spiritual traditions: the initiation of the spiritual hero. The story plots out the preparation for undertaking a spiritual life, and it chronicles the death of one's old attachments to the world, which must take place if a person is to take up another calling. Using the ear reserved for hearing the unspoken, you can hear in the story that there was a Fourth Temptation waiting for the young man Jesus in the lonely barrens of Galilee, though it did not survive the editing of the Synoptic Tradition.

We are told that Jesus was *led* out into the wilderness — out of the world — and was sorely tempted. We can assume from the word "led" that at the time it was not his choice to go to the wilderness, and he may not have seen it as a particularly good idea. He was tempted by daily bread — that is, by deliverance from bodily weakness — and he was dared to test God's relationship with him. The other temptation, naturally, was money and power, dominion over the whole world. Having mastered these temptations, and the Tempter as well, the story leaves him there, in some versions being rewarded for his endurance of the ordeal by ministering angels offering good nourishment. Having reached the *apogée* of his spiritual life — he had become the Spiritual Warrior that New Age literature describes — we might wonder why he would leave the field of his victory. Why would he rejoin the world of human commerce? I'm suggesting that he did not do so willingly.

The Fourth Temptation of Jesus was the temptation to sit tight, to stay in the desert like many of the early church patriarchs in Egypt did after him, to keep things simple: the sand, the sky, some daily bread, and his God. From a psychological point of view, Jesus had to be *driven back into town*, away from his competence and strength and his victories, away from his remove and his resolve and his noble aversions, and into the world again.

This is the way it is for the Spiritual Warrior. He or she tends to be more at home in the struggle of the vanquishing, not in the struggle of governance. There is something of a young person's game in that preference, an inclination away from the mundane and away from connectedness with the community. There is a distaste for the hurly burly, a nausea in the face of the unspectacular and the banal. Money, for all its attraction and mystery, is also so mundane and so irredeemably ordinary. And money has a way of nailing a person to the Wheel of this World. When you are with money, you are imbedded in this life, in the mundane, in the world of governance and getting.

There seems to be a great implacability here between the yearning for a spiritual life and the conditions of moneyed, communal life. Of course, Jesus had to be *driven* back into the world, where his vision would be tested by the marketplace, and so toward crucifixion. This is a psychological, spiritual, and historical fact — and it is one that each of us lives through in tireless cycles during our lives. It is not something that happens just once.

> *The world is too much with us; late and soon,*
> *Getting and spending, we lay waste our powers;*
> *Little we see in Nature that is ours;*
> *We have given our hearts away . . .*
> *It moves us not. Great God! I'd rather be*
> *A Pagan suckled in a creed outworn;*
> *So might I, standing on this pleasant lea,*
> *Have glimpses that would make me less forlorn . . .*[4]
> — WILLIAM WORDSWORTH, "THE WORLD IS TOO MUCH WITH US"

Wordsworth's lament is the lament of every life-encrusted, soul-enchanted human being who feels riven by the invitations of the Gods and the dispiriting demands of the madding crowd. A person so afflicted already has a foot in each world! Jesus stands in the midst of a long line of such heroic figures whose lives are paradigms of the crucial struggle of each man or woman toward authentic, soulful humanity. They are not models to be envied or imitated. They are frames of reference through which our own lives can be seen as a story, with plot, fate, moral, torment, redemption, and the rest. They are human stories through which The Human Story can be told, recognized, and retold.

Though he continues to be regarded in both secular and religious contexts as a heroic and otherworldly figure, Jesus had a human mind and soul, including the capacity for a vast and unconscious ambivalence. Consider the imprecation against rich men entering the Kingdom of God from this point of view. Injunctions of this kind, with their stiffening; their ruthless, aversive posture; their blackening of the enemy; their bristling rancour; are signs of an unwilling, unsuspected encounter of the self with the shadow of things. They are a confession of ambivalence disguised in the garb of unequivocation — as many such confessions are. Jesus might be having a hard time with rich people and with money here, though he puts a brave face on it. Of course, this perspective is influenced by the consideration that Jesus as a child would likely have suffered the dual indignity of being poor and being a bastard son in a time and culture where neither attribute was likely to have been particularly honoured or auspicious. That being so, he would certainly have been excluded from privilege, from ease, from material well-being. Perhaps his family's main money problem was that there wasn't enough. So he comes to the money problems as a have-not.

• • •

There are other stories in the Synoptic Tradition where Jesus appears to have sorted out the money-and-spirit question in richer terms that allow for the ambivalence toward money and privilege to stand — including perhaps his own ambivalence. The "render unto Caesar" story is one of these. We can imagine that his tolerance and endurance of ambivalence was achieved at considerable expense to him. The naïveté about money — the projections concerning intimacy, spirituality, and money, the envy of the rich and their privilege — which stands at the heart of so many darkened views of money, all of these things he would have to surrender, with more or less grace, if he partook of them, in order that the ambivalence about money might be explored and understood. Surrender, sacrifice, but not denial. Only in this way might some compassion in money matters prevail. In Jesus' case, the naïveté and the projections and the envy were surrendered by having endured an initiation that included real danger, real hardship and deprivation, and the possibility of real failure. After this initiation, Jesus seems to have undertaken a life that gave room for the ambivalences and complexities that help to define "the soul's way."

Tolerating and enduring these ambivalences are crucifixions of a kind. It is difficult to be torn between rages — say, between the rage to be right and the rage to feel good about being right. Necessity has its way with you when you are stretched out and nailed by inner conflicts like these, conflicts which so easily find their counterparts in the outer world. The poet Tim Lilburn wrote about this, covering the ground that separates fascination from crucifixion in a few lines:

> *Looking takes you so far on a leash of delight, then*
> *removes it and says*
> *the price of admission to further is your name.*
> *Either the desert . . . or a palace life . . . Choose.*[5]
> — "CONTEMPLATION IS MOURNING"

The cost of learning more is a sacrifice of your unconsidered, untested base sense of who you are — in Lilburn's phrase, "your name" and in our terms, "your self." In that sense, Jesus would have had to surrender the gestures of divestiture of and aversion toward money which are so seductive and, in the early going, so persuasive and so apparently true. When he answered the Pharisees' question "Is it right to pay taxes to Caesar or not?" with the enigmatic "Render unto Caesar what is Caesar's and what is God's unto God," he was keeping the money questions alive. He said, *You* answer the question. This invites the inquisitor to step backwards, by way of confessing his convictions about money, away from the self and toward his soul.

Jesus' greater wisdom in the matters of money and the life of the spirit, acquired in part through the struggles he might have had over his own kinship and over his purpose in being alive, is the gift he tried to give to those who may have thought they had cornered him in the labyrinth of projection, logic, legalism, and disavowal. Though they didn't suspect it (judging from the spirit of their questioning), Jesus seems to have given his inquisitors the chance to redeem money from the shadows and the opportunity to ennoble their theological speculations and their financial transactions with soulfulness.

• • •

I would read the warning about serving two masters in the same light. When Jesus says, "You cannot serve both God and Mammon," he is placing money in good company, is he not? This is subtle teaching, not a shaming epithet, and it is not a simple statement. Freud reminded us earlier that the word "Mammon" comes from a Babylonian phrase which described gold as the feces of hell. A literal and rational mind would hear this only as a deeply disparaging description of gold and money. But mythologically speaking, there are folktales the world over which tell that the search for gold usually leads to the dung heap. The gold in these tales is the soul's gold — the things a person must learn to live in a soulful way — and dung is a rich metaphor for that cast-off and disowned part of the soul which is the least tolerated and most intimate of our aversions. The offal is also the humus, not clean and not without offence, perhaps, but generative and pure.

Jesus might not be discrediting the magic of money by this comparison. He acknowledges that it is easy to confuse God and Mammon, because there is a kind of unsuspected kinship between the two. They are vast, provocative, otherworldly things — complex, demanding, and revelatory. The kinship is to be recognized, this teaching suggests, and not avoided. Sarcasm and irony are not at work here. The suggestion of some kinship between the mystery of God and the magic of money might harken back to an ancient period in humankind's understanding of Gods and Creation. There was a time, still accessible to us in our ancestral memories, when the wrinkled choreography of the world offered evidence that there were many Gods, with different functions and different domains. These Gods were often in conflict, and they contended for the attention and fidelity of humans. In the just, reciprocal ecology of spirit of those times, Gods and humans had mutually complementary needs: what one could do with ease, the other needed and could not do. It fell to human beings to see to it that each God received its due. You could not serve two Gods the same food. The requirements of each God had to be studied and learned, memorized and honoured, and human beings who served the good of the village and the world were charged with those tasks. Jesus might have been advocating the same kind of service in his time — a recognition that God and Mammon made different demands and that serious learning was needed to tell the differences.

Well, we are possibly in the land of idolatry here, and we should have something to say about idolatry in a book about money and the soul. We must understand that the modern period in North America has been the testing ground for a thorough program of desecration and demythologization. The Scientific Revolution, the Enlightenment, and the omnipresence of the psychological worldview have all made a considerable contribution to the discrediting and dismantling of the foundational stories of Judaeo-Christian culture, as well as to the wholesale war upon Indigenous cultures and their worldviews. Stories like the Garden of Eden, the Flood, the Virgin Birth, and the Resurrection have all been dismissed — deconstructed — as not being historical, or factual, or culturally relevant. In their place, we have hypotheses, concepts, theories, and complexes.

But these stories don't have to be historically accurate to be true. They are metaphors of birth, of the dawning of consciousness, of the loss of innocence, of the interweaving of life and death. This is a literalizing culture, and this culture does not understand or honour metaphor. The capacity to see these stories as the metaphors they are was lost when the culture surrendered to rationalism and literalism.

A person or a culture that has gone literal and lost the capacity for mythological thinking has also lost the ability to mediate experience. Such a person or culture is easily overwhelmed by trauma. On an individual level, a person diagnosed by psychiatry as having an obsessive-compulsive disorder is more adequately understood as a person who seeks relief from his or her palpable despair by returning again and again to routinized futility. This is a traumatized soul in rigid, involuntary, and inevitable genuflection to an inert and unresponsive God. And that is what idolatry is: the collapse of the imagination in the face of irreducible trauma. The result is fanatical, literal, continuous re-enactment by the self of an event it cannot *imagine* its way through. It is an act of propitiation which never buys absolution.

At a cultural level, the biblical story of the Israelites worshipping the golden calf during their desert wanderings is a clear example of the loss of the capacity for experiencing life metaphorically and the slide into idolatry. A wandering tribe, homeless after generations lived under an oppressive regime which took their stories away, uncertain of its future, the reliability of its old stories, or its leader, concretizes its trauma in the form of a golden figure from a foreign myth, moulded with what had been saved and hoarded and spirited out of captivity and melted down. This is not a tale about what money can do to a people. It can be read as a cautionary tale about how the loss of imagination and metaphor can make idols out of fears and out of what has been rejected or lost or forgotten.

A person struggling to find a place for money in the soul's life is struggling on behalf of metaphorical thinking and against idolatry. The soul is not an idol. The world-soul is not an idol. The Gods and spirits of the wild places are not idols. A soul unacknowledged and unimagined becomes an idol, a wounded, solitary effigy, shrouded and cornered. A world-soul neglected, polluted, and violated becomes an idol, hostile and remote to human beings. And Gods and spirits unmet, unloved,

149

and unfed by human beings become the ossified, haunted, and hungry beings manifest in mania, depression, and desecration. I was warned once: Don't confuse Creation with the Creator. It was intended as a warning against idolatry. But demeaning Creation doesn't guard against idolatry. Recognizing the soul of the world and our kinship with it is an antidote to idolatry.

• • •

We know that attendance at places of worship in the Western world is now lower than it has been at any point in modern times. It is safe to say that most people have no priest or minister or spiritual advisor that they engage on any kind of regular basis. Most people are likely to see a clergyperson as often as they see a tax preparer. So without clearly marked sacred places or sacred times or people who point us to the sacred, where are we to live our spiritual lives, and where are we to have our spiritual experiences and spiritual struggles? How are we to work on understanding mythological thinking, metaphor, and idolatry? With a diminished appreciation for the crucial importance of myth and metaphor and magic, how does a person even imagine the relevance of soulfulness?

The steep rise in the use of psychological counsellors over the last half-century is no doubt an attempt to find the same kind of guidance and solace once found with the clergy, without the "burden of tradition" to plough through. Alas, the counselling world is generally not well prepared to address the consequences of the trauma of literal, rational living, nor does it tend to support the yearning for a soulful approach to life. Many counsellors see the principal conflicts of life as raging within each person rather than between people, or between people and spirits, and thus they target the individual psyche as the place for intervention. That is why money is rarely discussed in psychological or pastoral counselling. In fact, the community life of which money is a part is largely ignored in the counselling world — and this is a dangerous omission. James Hillman and Michael Ventura were probably thinking about this when they wrote a book called *We've Had a Hundred Years of Psychotherapy and the World's Getting Worse*. This clever aphorism admirably points out: *You* might feel better, but tell me there's a benefit for the *world* in that. What is the cost to the world, in other words, of your fenced-in backyard staying emerald green in a late summer drought?

People engaged in psychotherapy usually have an intense and intimate relationship with the therapist. Intimacy first describes a relationship of proximity, not a relationship of preference. You can, for example, draw close to people in certain circumstances that you'd otherwise never consider spending time with. Intimacy doesn't suggest that you like the intimacy, or that you like the other person. It only suggests that you have drawn close to them. I know this experience both as a practitioner and as a recipient of psychotherapy. When training for the work, I sought out a therapist in order to become more aware of my "blind spots" and in order to know what it felt like to be on the other side. When I remember a particular teaching I received, it still makes me wince at the unconscious naïveté it revealed.

Shortly after I started therapy, the doctors where I lived undertook job action for the first time in their professional lives. This required every practitioner to negotiate with each patient the payment for services which were not covered by the government health insurance plan. In my case, I was being asked to pay a surcharge for services like prescription writing, collaboration with other professionals, telephone consultation, and the like — none of which I ever required. We discussed it at some length, and I agreed and signed accordingly, mainly to get the discussions over with. At this point, I felt that the money business was finally dealt with, and we could go back to our real business, the world of my inner life.

Now it was normal practice that once a month there would be a small, anonymous white envelope waiting for me on the corner of the psychiatrist's desk, with my bill in it. Nothing was ever said. I just picked it up upon leaving and returned it the next week with a cheque. Being a student at the time, the day came when I was short of money. The psychiatrist's bill wasn't a large amount, but there wasn't enough money to go around. So without thinking about it much, I attended the next session and before getting started said, "Oh yeah, about the bill. I'm a little short this week, so I hope it can wait until next session." I sat down and started to settle into my introspective face to get the session underway. Then I noticed that he was staring disconcertedly at the ground. He didn't respond at all to my offhand suggestion, and the awkward silence grew longer and louder. It was a moment of intense discomfort.

Without thinking, I presumed that this was an automatic solution, and that he'd just rubberstamp my offer, but he did not. When he finally broke the silence he said, "Why me?" In utter disbelief I stammered, "Pardon?" And he said it again, in a tone that mixed equal parts of curiosity and vague offence: "Why me? Why do I have to wait for the money?"

That psychiatrist put me through a brutal exposé of my naïveté and my unconsciousness around the whole business of money and intimacy with his two-word inquiry. Of course he could live without my small payment for a week, and of course he understood that students run out of money before they run out of month from time to time. But that wasn't his point. His point was, How did I decide to ask *him* to wait for the money, and not someone else? He taught me the way some zen abbots teach their shaven-headed acolytes, by engineering for me a painful and mostly wordless collision with my own unaware self. He knew, and he helped me to see, that I was trading on our familiarity in hopes that he would let the money thing slide, and that I was relying on him to do his part and say nothing but "okay." He refused to be complicit. After recovering from my feelings of ambush and betrayal, which might have taken some hours together, I actually felt closer to him, and more grateful, and I came to see, in his awkward silence, wisdom and a kind of compassion from him that I hadn't felt before. So there are times when good therapy brings soulfulness into the project of understanding the gawky, mumbling self.

● ● ●

Though I have not seen the report itself, I read recently about the results of a survey conducted among psychiatrists and analysts. The question put to them was along the lines of, What are the most inadvisable things you could engage in with a patient? What activity would be the most damaging to the course of therapy? What is the ultimate therapeutic taboo? Treating a relative or friend must have been on the list. Befriending a patient was probably on the list. Marrying a patient was on the list, no doubt. Of course, we would expect that having sex with a patient, say, or a patient's child or spouse, would be at the top, but it was not. "It was discovered that touching and holding, shouting and hitting, drinking, kissing, nudity and intercourse"[6] all fell behind something that was a greater taboo still. What was the ultimate transgression, the violation of trust which no therapeutic alliance could survive? *Lending the patient money.*

Surprised? By now, you shouldn't be. There actually is some kind of compassion floating around in this aversion. Therapists who respond to money questions in this way are trying to spare themselves and their clients a dilemma so confounding as to threaten the integrity and endurance of the therapeutic relationship. They don't want *that* kind of relationship with their clients. The therapeutic expectation is that the client should be able to handle such entanglements in the context of marital intimacy, and do so with skill. But they could never handle money mysteries in that other intimacy, the therapeutic intimacy.

These are entanglements which the container of therapeutic

intimacy, so intense, so covert, and so privileged, could never survive. Many therapists practise Old Order Psychology, keeping the Caesar of money and the God of the soul separate. Jesus, who with more modest aspirations might have made a good and radical psychologist, saw the utter necessity of keeping them bound together.

Money is the prodigal son of therapy. Therapy must go to money and embrace it like a lost child. Spiritually inclined people and seekers of all kinds must contend well with other people's money and with other people's poverty. They must, more importantly, befriend their own uneasiness about their own money, or lack of it. If not, writes psychologist James Hillman,

the soul is deflected onto a spiritual path of denial and the world is left in the sins of luxuria, avarice and greed. [For] money is the place where God and Caesar divide [and this] shows that money is a "third thing" like the soul itself, and that in money are both the inherent tendency to split into spirit and matter and the possibility to hold them together.[7]

Finally, there's a short meditation on the confluence of money and the life of the spirit that is given to us by the Persian poet Rumi, who was a founder of the ecstatic branch of Islam known as the Dirvishes. It's clear from his poetry that he was an immensely playful and fierce man, and his teachings always seem to include a precise and demanding eye.

These spiritual windowshoppers,
who idly ask, How much is that? Oh, I'm just looking.
They handle a hundred items and put them down,
interest with no capital.
What is spent is love and two eyes wet with weeping.
But these walk into a shop,
and their whole lives pass suddenly in that moment,
in that shop.

Where did you go? "Nowhere."
What did you have to eat? "Nothing much."

Even if you don't know what you want,
Buy something, to be part of the exchanging flow.[8]

Rumi's poem asks, What are you saving yourself for? I love that unexpected imprecation, to buy *something*. It is not the kind of spiritual direction you might expect. He says, become ensnared in this world, so you won't be a stranger to entanglement, so that you won't fear it, so you may be capital and not shadow. He does not counsel aloofness or purity or a life in the desert. He says, *Spend your soul.*

Forgiveness

To live outside the law you must be honest.
— Bob Dylan

By the time I went to university I had worked out most of the God and Man questions and the spiritual quandaries to my utter satisfaction. God was a concept developed to account for all those inexplicable things that befall us, and the soul was the place in us that fretted unnecessarily over them. With that arrogant certainty firmly in place, I took a year off from my religious studies program when I was twenty-one or so and did the mandatory tour of Europe. After stowing away on a Greek luxury liner out of Malaga, Spain, I jumped ship in Gibraltar and worked there for a time as a stone mason. Sometimes I played and sang in a bar at night for people who were, luckily for me, more enamoured with, than knowledgeable about, North American folk music. All of this bought me more time in Europe, since I didn't have much money. Then I joined the crew of a noble, leaky, nineteenth-century ketch bound for Malta. A week into the voyage we were caught by a thirty-hour, force-eleven gale. The sails and rudder were ravaged, and what was left of us was blown hopelessly off course. At the worst of it, we were hand bailing a sixty-eight-foot boat to stay afloat. The smallest man had to crawl into the bilge among the rats and the diesel fumes to begin the bailing line — and I'm still not very tall. A slow but certain death was a real possibility, and there were nervous breakdowns and madnesses of all kinds among the small crew, bless their souls. Machado's advice about the fear of going down being useless at sea would have been dark comfort, had I known it then. Many in the crew were demented — and maybe changed forever — by their fear of an event that never came to pass. There were hours of daylight and darkness in the howling grip of the gale spent imagining the last minutes, the last seconds, the last breath of our lives, and through those hours, hardly a word was passed among us.

There were other mishaps, but we were rescued and then arrested by the Sicilian coast guard in Palermo. At their request, Interpol became involved, as we were suspected of being a hopeless international band of incompetents who'd gotten into a mess while running drugs or guns to the Middle East. We were each interrogated at length. The lone woman on board, a Spaniard, was asked by a puffed-up Sicilian navy man, "What were you doing out there with those wolves?" She shot him a look, and with some exaggeration, said, "They're not wolves. They're perfect gentlemen." After living under machine-gun guard for a few days, we were suddenly released without explanation. It took me only minutes to pack up and leave the boat, the harbour, and the country. Physically and emotionally wrecked after the ordeal, I took a train to Paris and wandered for several days with little money and no prospects, trying to get my bearings.

Paris, I found, was a city just too old and too worldly for a semi-destitute and exhausted North American kid. One day, as I wandered aimless and apprehensive, I was approached by at least seven beggars on the streets looking for money. I was becoming increasingly hostile at this intrusion. I could say that my hostility came from my exhaustion or my broken-down public-school French or from the fact that I had little money, but the truth was that I felt preyed upon and resentful and victimized by these people. I was offended by them, by their intrusions, by having to deal with the business of not *wanting* to give them anything, over and over again. I took refuge in, fittingly, Notre Dame Cathedral. I knew something of the history of the place, and I took a seat in the middle of the nave, away from all the gaping, pointing, mumbling tour groups. Once I'd calmed down a little, I sat there in awe at the grandeur of it all, and the folds of ceremony and history rustled all around me. There I was, a shipwrecked, gaunt, tenaciously adolescent kid from the New World, in Notre Dame. For a moment, I was lost in wonder and relief, and I loved life.

In the middle of this reverie, a man suddenly appeared at my left. I did not see him approach. He was in early middle age and a bit threadbare, but not poorly dressed — in shades of grey — with a strange brightness in his eyes. He smilingly asked for a few francs, which if I remember rightly was less than a half-dollar in those days. My reverie ground to a halt, my heart knotted again, and I was ready, Crusader style, for a righteous conflict. I summoned my mediocre French and scolded him in a disgusted way. "It isn't proper to beg in a church," I declared. (I believe it came out that way.) Then I looked off into the middle distance with indignation and a thin, dismal feeling of propriety. He gave me a half-bow from the waist, smiled, took four steps backwards without taking his eyes from me, and disappeared into the ether.

As surely as I sit here now and tell this story, he was there one second and gone the next. I was dazed about this for a long time afterwards — years. Only slowly did I come to conclude — what else could it have been? — that an angel had come to me in Notre Dame Cathedral. At that time, I had what was and probably still is the typical North American's unexamined view that giving money to beggars only encourages them to beg. The only way to break them of the "habit" was to stand your ground and encourage or shame them back to self-sufficiency. This defence against the need of others was and is really a defence against the *presence* of others. It is a posture so thorough in its blindness that there is almost no challenge possible, no chink in the armour. So, apparently, I needed an angel to break this isolated arrogance and touch me with the humanity of the Other Person. It seems I needed to learn a little humility about alms giving, and something about money and the soul's desires.

• • •

The English language, like all mongrels, is tenacious and sullen when it is not accommodating. The words we use to describe money and the words we use to deal in it are from the Old World for the most part. It is early mediaeval Christendom, not Microsoft, that has given us our money language. Those double-edged activities we spoke of earlier — redemption, reconciliation, covenant, and forgiveness — can all be engaged in with equal facility and gravity in a bank, a boardroom, or a place of worship or contemplation. Joseph Campbell, the well-known myth scholar, has said that the Church borrowed its language from the moneylenders. This may be, and if so, it has created a confounding debt that the church has not yet paid off. No matter which came first, the flowing together of money and spirituality in language, which the centuries have been unable to separate, has so far proven to be a worthy topic for our interest and examination.

Our concern in this chapter is to come to some good understanding of the convolutions of indebtedness, trespass, and forgiveness. My own story about the angel is an example of how money can flush into the open all these covert fears and prejudices about having and giving and owing and belonging.

Westerners generally place a high premium on freedom from financial and emotional indebtedness, and we invoke that "freedom" as the principal means of maintaining healthy relationships with family, friends, and strangers. I am going to challenge this idea that a "clean" relationship, free from indebtedness, is a good one. I am going to challenge the morbid existentialist mantra that says, Hell is other people.

A debt is an occasion to observe the kinship of money and spiritual practice made manifest. We have three choices to make after debts are incurred: they can be discharged, they can be ignored, or they can be forgiven. We ought not to overlook the confluence of forgiveness and indebtedness. There is considerable wisdom about this in the anarchic, fiscally dicey supplication we call the Lord's Prayer.

> Give us today the bread we need for today,
> and forgive the debts we owe you. And
> we'll forgive the debts owed us by others.

The prayer allows that having basic needs met — having daily bread — makes it easier for people to forgive the debts and grudges they might hold against another person. It is easier because forgiveness will come from a full belly or a full pocket and a feeling of amplitude, surplus, and security that the universe is unfolding as it should. This is a very iffy proposition, however — to *hope* to have the bread you need for today and to give up the right to any debt owed you. Daily life — the one that I know, at least — seems to teach that to secure the bread for today and tomorrow, you have to get paid or paid back first. We seem to tempt the Gods of mischief, poverty, and mayhem by saying this kind of prayer out loud.

Discharging a debt is really the easy part, regardless of one's fiscal health, because it asks the least, spiritually speaking, of either party. Presuming that the nature and breadth of the debt is clear, paying it off is a self-evident business, and it is fact and not opinion that it has been paid. Ignoring a debt, well, that will ensnare those involved in the transaction, drawing them into wider and meaner rings of resentment or guilt. Ignorance of this kind accumulates a tortured psychological, financial, and spiritual interest that can hardly be spoken, much less paid. Neglect compounds the interest on a debt, and it can spell the end of many relationships. But for all this mayhem, ignoring a debt is not hard to do. With all the dishonest, envious convolutions of the mind that people are exposed to, ignoring debts happens every day, all day long.

Forgiveness of a debt is, surprisingly, the thorniest of these undertakings because it is the most difficult one to do well. There are two prerequisites for forgiving, whether the question is one of a money debt or an emotional trespass. The first prerequisite is confession; the other is discernment. In my counselling work, I often see people who will forgive in a pre-emptive way. This is a particular problem for people from faith communities. Forgiveness is often automatic for these people — a reflexive gesture and a credal expectation. A person who forgives in this way wants to forgive the offender before the offender is aware of the offence and before any confession is made. Forgiving this way is often used as a strategy for not letting the ugly thing — the trespass, the indebtedness, in all its angry, sullen glory — emerge from the shadows. When that happens, forgiveness is not much more than a noble gesture put in the service of numbness or forgetfulness or neglect. People who forgive like that have bathed in the river Lethos, and they say to others, "Come on in. The water's fine." When the confession is absent, when the forgiveness comes in before the confession struggles out, nothing happens. Without the opportunity to confess, the one forgiven is left asking the bewildered question, "What have I been forgiven for?" And the benefactor, the one "forgiving," is complicit in keeping the trespass mute, unacknowledged, and unconscious.

The well-intentioned forgiving person will say, "Honestly, don't mention it. That's OK. Don't worry, don't feel bad. It's nothing, really. Forget about it." These might be lovely sounds to the one who owes the debt, especially if he or she is tormented by the indebtedness more than by the debt. But I question whether the one who forgives in this way is really a benefactor. To whose benefit does this pre-emptive forgiveness run? Not letting the confession out can easily become a way of driving the supplicant further into indebtedness. Real forgiving proceeds first from the debtor fessing up to what he or she has done, to what he or she owes, and *to his or her capacity to incur and endure indebtedness*. Real forgiveness requires the one to whom the debt is owed to confess to what he or she has let the debtor do to them, and *to their own capacity to indulge and prolong indebtedness* by not acknowledging it. Debtor and debtee are bound together not only by the debt, but also by this "gravitational pull" by which the deep machinations of forgiveness compel them. The debt, or the trespass, if it is to be truly forgiven, makes demands on both partners.

Debts incurred between family members, where bloodlines are traded upon to soften or obscure indebtedness, are tortuous because the confession usually doesn't occur at all. The family will decide, covertly, that indebtedness is hostile to the bonds of family life. That is the real disaster of monetary or emotional debt in family life: not that there is debt, but that the debt isn't articulated.

In fact, true forgiveness *has* to be overt. Forgiveness has to be recognized and acknowledged with eloquence — in its revisiting of the scene of the indebtedness and in its embrace of the thing forgiven. A little eloquence in confession is warranted, eloquence in confessing a trespass or in receiving the confession of one. Things must be said, and said well, to be recognized by both parties. Well-spokenness in confession touches the heart of both, and it conjures a heady mix of humiliation, tenderness, acknowledgement, and peace. People who feel themselves limited in their ability to express themselves well have some work to do. So do verbose people who speak but do not act. Eloquence in confession serves up the feast of restitution.

The second prerequisite for forgiving is discernment. An important question you should ask yourself is this: Should I forgive this debt? In whose interest is it to forgive the debt? Or should I *accept* such forgiveness of a debt owed by me when it is offered by the one I owe or have trespassed against? This is an especially important question to ask yourself if this forgiveness is something you long for. In that longing, there is usually much shadow. I remember during my growing up years how the adults around me used to sneer indignantly at the Catholic institution of confession and penance. Later, people my own age did this too. They seemed to think that Catholic confession was too easy, too glib. It was irresponsible. They found it ludicrous that just saying something about a trespass did something about it. It too much resembled a kind of deal, and yet it cost nothing — which is akin to complaining that a restaurant's food is not only bad, but that it comes in such small servings. I grew up convinced that confession was essentially impure and unbecoming, a charade of the resolution of indebtedness. You could hear in this sneer the deep misgivings the elders around me had when dealings with God too much resembled transactions between people. Too much calculation, they said, too much like business. So Protestant Orangemen of that time felt a lot of ambivalence about being too calculating or discerning or direct in their spiritual affairs, preferring to abandon those talents when approaching the church doors. And they were content to let the Catholics labour under their fallacy, and to let them carry their sooted misgivings about money and its connections to the spiritual life for the rest of us. As my time in Notre Dame showed, I learned their lessons well. The ridicule of Catholic confession, it turned out, blinded us to the vital role that confession has to play in human relationships.

Those who share this ambivalence will work hard to keep money matters and spiritual matters separate by not engaging the shadowy business dredged up by confession and discernment. The business of indebtedness then has no spiritual discipline, and it is a snarling or empty or humiliating transaction. Then there is a small echo, from a hollow place, when we redeem a bond, reconcile an account, forgive a debt. Nothing really happens. All that is left to say is that you are now on the hook or now off the hook. But forgiveness and the desire to be forgiven are much more complex than that.

What is the source of the strong desire to be free from debt? The answer is probably too obvious if you think only of money debts. But if you ask the same question of emotional debts, the challenge is clear: why would a person — a whole culture — yearn for a relationship that is so well balanced that nobody owes anybody anything? The language of indebtedness — redemption, reconciliation, covenant, grace, forgiveness — offers us a chance for conscious awareness of what is really at stake, and it presents us with a way of approaching both kinds of debt in a soulful fashion.

• • •

A few years ago in Toronto a bedraggled young woman appeared in a police station with a woeful tale. It seemed that she was in the end stages of cancer. She was a stranger in the city and had with her a fatherless seven-year-old son about to be orphaned. A recent mugging and robbery had left her penniless, without her prescription drugs, and minus the one-way bus ticket to Winnipeg she'd bought for the boy to use once she had died. She had nothing. It was a story of bottomless woe. Even the police, who had pretty much heard it all, were moved to action. It appears they alerted the media, perhaps without the woman's knowledge, and the media — no surprise — loved the story. The subsequent publicity resulted in a local bank starting a fund for the woman and her son. Within a week the public donations got up over $110,000, and then to $140,000. The giving was unprecedented. Nothing in living memory in that city compared to the spontaneity and the magnitude of the public response to one person's need. The swelling bank balance for the mystery woman and her son became another fabulous news story, and the city's generosity yet another. Everyone, it seemed, felt good, and everyone was doing good. There wasn't a shadow in the story anywhere.

One important detail should be borne in mind: so far as I know, the woman is not on record as ever having publicly asked for money. She never did plead her case in the marketplace. People came forward in the way that they did without any request for personal assistance from her, which seemed like a lovely thing at the time. The police and the media cooperated in maintaining her anonymity, and they drove the story relentlessly. Everyone — the woman and her son, the police, the media, the bank, the public at large — was a hero.

After several days, the woman made a videotape. She appeared only in silhouette, and in a beautiful, delicate, and unrehearsed way thanked the people of the city for their extraordinary generosity and for keeping her anonymity and integrity intact. This short address was broadcast by all the local television stations. By now, this ultimate good news story was known across the country, and beyond. The woman was quite eloquent in her address, and she concluded her appreciation by saying, "Please don't send any more money. It's enough now."

It's doubtful that the media would have let the story end there, with the woman quietly dying and her son taking that bus to Winnipeg, with his education bankrolled. As it turned out, the reporters didn't have long to wait for further developments. Though her face was blacked out, her voice and story were recognized by a former common-law husband who'd seen the broadcast. He contacted the police. Within a day or two, a sad history of this woman's pathological lying and convictions for public mischief came to light. The gist of her story was found to be a fabrication. There was some illness, but doctors who were brought in Inquisition style, as were the priests and bishops to Joan of Arc to decide the veracity of her claims, stated flatly that her demise was far from imminent. The bank account was frozen. The woman was identified to the media, fingerprinted, photographed, and charged. It appears the police made a particular point of trooping this fallen angel in front of cameras and microphones. After being charged, the woman was left to walk the long walk from the police station doors to a waiting station-wagon alone, without the cordon of anonymous credibility supplied earlier by her protectors and advocates. The cameras whirred and snapped, the TV stations got their film, and the reporters fell over each other trying to pry a word from her. She refused further comment, and was gone.

For days afterwards, media people met on each other's talk shows castigating themselves for their handling of the whole thing, for their naïveté and for their lack of suspicion, and they spent time on the street asking people their reaction to these events. The most commonly asked questions were "Do you feel betrayed? Will this make you think twice about giving to charity in the future?" — which gives some indication of how the media people themselves were feeling.

• • •

To understand what really happened there, and to bring a soulful approach to that story, we need some understanding about charity. Almsgiving is an antique word in our culture, but the spiritual and financial struggles which attend the issue of deciding how and to whom to give — and the debt such giving creates — are very much with us. The mediaeval Jewish jurist Maimonides developed quite an elaborate system for sorting out the difficult business of tithing, charity, and the giving of alms. He described a method that connected tithing to spiritual reward or achievement — including several scenarios promising ever-increasing levels of spiritual reward and enlightenment for alms givers and receivers alike. The first scenario, the one most limited in its efficacy and spiritual valence, was one in which the donor and the supplicant were known to each other, each familiar with the other's need or surplus, each present at the exchange of the gift, each managing as best they could the awkwardness and the humbling, the projections and the shame and the clumsy gratitude of the transfer of money or goods. The relationship established by the money in this kind of transaction is one principally between the obligation of the giver and the indebtedness of the receiver.

The last level is the zenith of spiritual and financial charity. In this most ennobling of transactions, the donor and the supplicant are unknown to each other. There is no subject for the gift and no object for the supplication. The giver surrenders any right to determine the destination of the alms and any right to learn after the fact where the money or the gift has gone. The community mediates the transaction. The alms pass through the community, as does whatever gratitude it arouses, and the community shares in the accrued spiritual interest. Brotherhood is alive in our midst, it says, and fellow sojourners are being cared for. The genius of this arrangement is that the acts of giving and receiving are public, and the benefits are public. The benefits are not restricted to the two principals. The movement of a gift in this way can broaden the circle of brotherhood while leaving the individuals their dignity. It is a reward which any gift exchange between three parties or more might normally generate.

Maimonides must have seen a need for offering a system that distributed the merits of almsgiving, along with the alms, over the whole community. He saw that anonymity was crucial to developing and maintaining the connection between money and the spiritual life. By removing the specific face of giver and receiver, almsgiving can reveal and manage the projective impulse in people. It confronts each participant in the exchange with the needs and assumptions which *they* bring to the encounter, but it does not transfer those needs and assumptions along with the alms.

The mechanics of this kind of almsgiving are subtle. The anonymity is an obligation of all parties partaking in the gift. The giver is unknown to the recipient, and vice versa. The anonymous gift, which almost seems to have anticipated the need of the recipient, stirs more than just passive reception. Alms might have the power to compel the recipient to respond actively to the gift. The recipient might have to contend, for instance, with the distinct possibility that the universe is a compassionate place and a friendly place, or that their needs or prayers have been answered in some way even if the prayer wasn't spoken. Those without a conscious instinct for prayer might have their rationalist view of the universe or their skepticism corrupted, which wouldn't be the worst thing that could befall them.

The giver might also become a recipient in this transaction. True, he or she doesn't receive accolades or thanks from the beneficiary. Instead, the giver receives the more subtle invitation to be content with the knowledge that a necessary thing has been done, though he or she will not be able to know the impact on the receiver's life. Instead, the consequences of almsgiving for the giver take place within the giver. Ultimately, this might bring the giver an opportunity to see up close his or her motivation for giving in the first place, and maybe to do a bit of pardoning of themselves for the self-interest that is sometimes part of giving.

This kind of almsgiving also prepares the participants to trade places by acquainting them anonymously with the tasks of their opposite number. A friend of mine objected to this idea and pointed out the problems with what he called "auto-pilot charity," when personal motivation and participation in the giving of alms is nonexistent. And he's right to object, because it is not inevitable that spiritual reward and insight flow from giving alms. Preferably, a contributor has to do *something* to accompany the gift he or she gives, and hopefully, the feeling of obligation and opportunity which the circle of charity stirs is not satisfied and numbed and cancelled by writing a cheque.

Spiritual discipline has a presence in the marketplace when gifts circulate. It turns the participants back to themselves, to witness their own soul's arousal in the presence of the received gift or in the possibility of giving. Giving like this means you do not control where your gift goes, nor what significance it has for someone else, nor what you may reap from giving. The givers, no less than the receivers, submit themselves to something more than their own ethics or ideas, motivation or experience, and more than obligation or tradition.

Many religious traditions stress the importance of sincerity in almsgiving. The word "sincere" comes from the Latin, meaning "without wax." Being an old stone carver, I find this etymology is close to my heart. There are many grades of marble. The porous ones are honeycombed with holes left by traces of other kinds of rock trapped in the cooling marble, and they are frowned upon by sculptors, masons, and architects. The old practice was to hide the holes in this poor man's marble with wax tinted to blend with the stone's colour. It takes a trained eye to spot the holey marble when it has been doctored in this way. Sincere marble lets the holes show, and sincere people taken up into the circulation of alms do the same.

There are two sources of reward in alms giving. One lies in the nature of the thing given, and the other in the size of the circle which the giving itself makes. I submit that the movement of some article from one person to another and then back again in kind, a trafficking in commodities, is a dead-end proposition. Take, as an example, the typical office Christmas party arrangement. Everyone draws a name so that everyone is included and no favourites are allowed, but the amount to be spent is carefully circumscribed. Why? Because the only permissible relationship between peers is a balanced relationship, where at the end of the exchange nobody owes anybody anything. And why is that important? Because indebtedness in relationships is almost intolerable in our culture, and most people scramble to get the account to zero as soon as possible — or they hold a mighty grudge if the account is not balanced in a timely fashion. These are not gifts, they are weights in the tray, balancing the relationship to nothing. The giver may have honourable motivations about reciprocity and grace in awkward situations, but that is of no consequence here. The desire to keep relationships simple, balanced, and unencumbered is not honourable. It is fear-driven, futile, and impoverishing of all who participate. "There is neither motion nor emotion [in commodity exchange] . . . the whole point is to keep the balance, to make sure the exchange itself doesn't consume anything or involve one person with another. Consumer goods are consumed by their owners, not by their exchange."[1] This can happen between friends; it can happen in a marriage.

● ● ●

A folk tale collected by the Grimm brothers warns pretty clearly of the perils of this closed and exclusive giving, and about the "hunger that appears when the gift stops moving."

> Once a man and his wife were sitting outside the front door with a roast chicken before them which they were going to eat between them. Then the man saw his old father coming along and quickly took the chicken and hid it, came, had a drink, and went away.
>
> Now the son was about to put the roast chicken back on the table, but when he reached for it, it had turned into a big toad that jumped in his face and stayed there and didn't go away again. And if anyone tried to take it away, it would give them a poisonous look, as if about to jump in their faces, so that no one dared touch it. And the ungrateful son had to feed the toad every day, otherwise it would eat part of his face. And thus he went ceaselessly hither and yon about in the world.[2]

175

The story clearly says it: any generosity built between two at the expense of, or to the exclusion of, the wider community is bound to shrivel up. You need a third person to make the gift nourishing. That gruesome image of the insatiable toad threatening to eat the man's face, and the fear and distaste preventing anyone from coming close or helping out, describes pretty well the disfigurement and isolation that will accrue to a controlled and exclusive friendship or marriage, where the emotional and spiritual gifts are kept indoors, out of the neighbourhood. The threat to others — that the toad will eat your face if you come too close — is a brilliant detail. Any helper is dissuaded by the distinct possibility that this disfigurement is contagious. It also describes the loneliness that grows in a marriage which turns in on itself and leaves out the larger community of in-laws, elders, neighbours, and all those who witnessed the wedding. The story warns that this particular husband and wife were afflicted forever with loneliness and isolation, even though they were together. I especially like the use of the word "ceaselessly" in the story, because it gives a good feeling for the insatiable hunger — physical and spiritual — that creeps into the house and cannot be fed.

So when you receive a gift, your obligation is not exclusively or even significantly to the giver, but to someone not yet included in the transaction, someone the first giver may never meet or know about. You can reciprocate, but that's not likely to change much in the relationship. There is a Middle Eastern proverb that says, If you want to own a man, give him a gift. That indentured servitude works only if both parties believe in

176

a balanced relationship, free of debt. If not, if the receiver passes along some of the gift, there is no prison at all — only community. Relationship and its spiritual wrinkles are evoked when the gift moves on, and when it gathers in neighbours and strangers alike by its movement. The bringing of a third person into the transaction of gift giving makes a circle instead of a line. It creates a little distance between giver and receiver by disturbing the delicate balance of mutual obligation, and in so doing it changes their relationship profoundly. Widening the circle creates a crucible for gratitude, and there is some wonder aroused when a gift comes in your door later, unannounced. The circulation of a gift over a greater and greater distance dissolves the smaller concentric egos of those involved and makes some room for the unexpected. It can *make* brotherhood and sisterhood, it can make for fellow-feeling. It can rattle the old unexamined commonness or mutual reciprocity that can burden so many intimate relationships and friendships. That is a function of gift exchange. It helps people find each other. That is why the giving of gifts is a fundamental element in peace making, for example.

This poem by Rilke has a good feel for the widening of the self and the stirring of the soul. The movement from the self to the community, as we have seen earlier, is a cornerstone for becoming a human being.

I live my life in growing orbits
which move out over the things of the world.

Perhaps I can never achieve the last.
but that will be my attempt.

I am circling around God, around the ancient tower,
and I have been circling for a thousand years,
and I still don't know if I am a falcon, or a storm,
or a great song.³

Martín Prechtel, an American man of Aboriginal and European background, was adopted into a Mayan village in Guatemala in the 1960s. The story of his stumbling into the village in search of a home, his introduction into the language and culture, and his eventual initiation as a shaman in the service of the village is a beautiful, lustrous one. He has written extensively about those experiences, and he argues intensely — he might say, harangues — for the redemptive power of the slumbering Indigenous soul waiting in every human being for recognition. In a book called *Long Life, Honey in the Heart*, Prechtel leaves what might be the most profound and most deceptively simple of his teachings for the last chapter. He describes how his responsibilities as a shaman required him to go into hopeless debt to other villagers to provide the material necessities for countless offerings and feasts. Later on, when he was able to make some money from selling his paintings, he brought the proceeds to pay back some of the elders in the village into whose debt he had so deeply, irrevocably fallen. To his dismay and utter befuddlement, he was met with verbal and physical attacks by these old men and women. When things calmed down enough to talk, he was asked, "What's wrong with you anyway? Don't you want to be one of us? All of a sudden you want to be alone, an orphan again?"

Prechtel was taught that what his people called *Kas-limaal*, mutual indebtedness, is the lifeblood of village life. It has two purposes: the first is to give all people a deep understanding of their kinship with each other and to offer them a way of living that kinship; the second is to make them taste their kinship with Creation, to think and feel and live as Creation lives. Hopeless entanglement in debt to all, Prechtel found, is the feeling tone of all natural life. An old man told him: "To get out of debt means you don't want to be part of life, and you don't want to grow into an adult." "Initiated youth are only half-cooked," writes Prechtel.

> They make babies, feed families and struggle for air, maybe succeeding at rising above others with mounds of goods, in debt to no one, giving to no one outside their own.
>
> You can only properly buy your way out of village indebtedness by more service . . . The idea is to get so entangled in debt that no normal human can possibly remember who owes whom what, and how much. In our business dealings, we keep close tabs on all exchanges, but in sacred dealings we think just like nature, where all is entangled and deliciously confused, dedicated to making the Earth flower in a bigger plan of spirit beyond our minds and understandings.[4]

Prechtel goes on to say that at the moment when he met the elders' objections, he understood their need of him and his need of them. He says that "they beseeched me not to kill their lives with my arrogance and modern independence." When this impossible-to-dispute wisdom of messy debt living got through to him, he became a true village man, a person, a human being, finally at home and belonging.

• • •

So what became of the woman who wandered into a Toronto police station with a good story to tell, and what can that story teach? Well, she was an angel, of a kind. Whatever she intended, she brought chaos to the order of that old, formalized, tired, and dispirited transaction between needy, worthy supplicant and noble, charitable almsgiver. This chaos-bringing is something that angels do well. Her half-appearance through the media prompted a widening of the charity circle. In fact, her half-appearance was *crucial* for that widening circle to grow. Her personal motivation, though poked at repeatedly in the subsequent news reports, was irrelevant to the story. And it surely had nothing to do with why people sent in their $10 and their $50, since she, it turned out, was unknown to all who gave. *Why* she did what she did had not much effect on how the story unfolded. The translation of compassion, pity, and "There but for the grace of God go I" into money by the readers and viewers drove the story. But the real story, the one the media missed entirely, was the arousal stirred in the almsgivers. The people who sent money to the bank thought they were giving it to a dispossessed cancer patient and her son. They thought they were redeeming a debt incurred on their behalf by the punks who'd robbed her or the cancer that was ravaging her or the brute unfairness of her son's impending orphanhood or the ornery and implacable melancholy of this world. But they were not. Nor were they giving money to someone who had explicitly asked for it.

Once this was revealed, once the woman and her motives were exposed and dissected, once the worthiness of the supplicant was corrupted and discarded, the contributors to the fund were faced with a painful dilemma. Did the purity of their impulse to give depend on the purity of the mysterious woman? If so, the nobility of the gesture fades more than a little bit, since the importance of the *giver's* motivation shrinks to nil. If not, then what about that bank account? What was to become of the money given? If she was a fallen angel after all, then it might follow that she was not entitled to a dime. Does the giver reclaim it and cease to be a giver? If so, a confession is made about their own motivation in giving, something of their need to be involved only in a safe and noble enterprise. Does the woman's charade — and the city's spasm of benevolence — ridicule, impugn, or disqualify the impulse to give? She was often portrayed as a seducer, and many people responded as though their simple and pure desire to help had been betrayed. But the real seducer was the invitation to cynicism and jadedness. Where was the betrayal?

What this woman did was to give the people of Toronto and all who heard the story a chance to engage the giving of money — whether they were givers themselves, or curious bystanders to the transaction — as a spiritual project. This opportunity presented itself only when the assumed purity of her actions was called into question, only when the chaos of the good city's revealed assumptions was brought into the ordered transaction of mutual need and mutual fulfilment. She didn't play the part of worthy supplicant in this exchange, and so she revealed much more about the spiritual conundrum of charity than she revealed about her own proclivity to embellish or invent her life story or con other people. In this way the woman did for the connection between money and the spiritual life what Jesus did two millennia ago: she did not resolve the ambivalence we have, and must have, about money and about the instincts of benevolence. She did not tell people what to do with their money — except to tell them, eventually, to stop sending it. She, by actions inadvertent, *insisted on the ambivalence that curls around money*, and in so doing that ambivalence came forward. The holes showed. Citizens were given the opportunity to bring to this and to other moneyed transactions the quality of soul. Ambivalence, conscious ambivalence, is a characteristic of soulfulness. The question raised by this woman's actions is: Who is my neighbour? So the whole contorted and disappointing mess conjured the principal conditions necessary for forgiveness: confession and discernment. Of course, she didn't mean to do this — and, of course, that changes nothing.

The story had an impossibly happy ending. Few people called to reclaim their contribution, some of it went to the woman's son, and before being distributed among many local charities, there it remained, a cache of $100,000 with no name on it, like the empty Ark of the Covenant, waiting to again be translated into conviction or into resentment, into betrayal or into compassion, into soulless indignation or into kinship. Inside a fiasco of big-city charity, the tangled garden of village indebtedness survived.

Conclusion
Breathing Deep the Fragrance of This World

Pablo Neruda, a soulful man who became a senator for his country and a poet to the whole world, grew up in a dingy backwater town in southern Chile at the beginning of the last century. His family was typical for that time and place, and his childhood was one of substantial material poverty. One day while playing behind his house he found a hole in the fence. He went to the hole and looked through it. Neruda was surprised to see a pasture and woods he'd somehow never noticed before. He played there by himself, and then for some reason stepped back from the fence for a moment. Suddenly, a boy's hand reached through the hole, laid a little toy sheep in the grass in front of him, and disappeared.

Neruda ran to the hole and looked through, but he saw no one. So he ran inside his house to get a prized possession of his own, a large fragrant pine cone, to exchange through the hole. He left it on the pasture side of the hole. He never saw the hand or the boy it belonged to again.

Neruda has written that this mysterious event, which shimmers and glows there like a true story about angels in the world, lies at the heart of all of his poetic and political work. This mystery gave him his feeling for wonder, redemption, and fraternity. It gave him his conscience.

> This exchange of gifts — mysterious — settled deep inside
> me like a sedimentary deposit
>   I have been a lucky man. To feel the intimacy of brothers
> is a marvellous thing in life. To feel the love of people
> whom we love is a fire that feeds our life. But to feel the
> affection that comes from those whom we do not know,
> from those unknown to us, who are watching over our sleep
> and solitude, over our dangers and weaknesses, that is
> something still greater and more beautiful because it widens
> out the boundaries of our being, and unites all living things.
>   That exchange brought home to me for the first time a
> precious idea: that all humanity is somehow together . . .
> It won't surprise you then that I have attempted to give
> something resiny, earthlike, and fragrant in exchange for
> human brotherhood . . .[1]

Neruda's worldwide notoriety and the adulation that came his way in the latter part of his life was a source of wonder to him. The statesman-poet was sage enough to know that he did not receive the gift of brotherhood simply because he deserved it. Neruda had a naturally keen eye for metaphor. From his own childhood isolation and deprivation, he recognized the material and spiritual poverty of the isolated, desolate cultures of the Americas. The hole in the fence was the wound in each desolate soul and in the soul of the rationalist, market-driven, and dangerously unconscious monocultures of these Americas. The mysterious gift, neither asked for nor merited nor imagined, comes through that hole, through the sorrow or the deprivation or deep confusion of the soul, and it is manifest proof of kinship with brothers and sisters unmet, with the vast parts of Creation unvisited, and with a world unseen, a world of spirit presences. Kinship — not sameness — is needed by individuals, cultures, and Creation. It is a material, political, cultural, and spiritual need of this world and of all things that live. The gift stirs this need in individuals and cultures, and unlike advertising, it honours and feeds that need. Neruda's soul recognized the gift that came to him through the hole in his fence, and he served it well by passing it on.

● ● ●

In this meditation, I have tried to offer a way of thinking about the dilemmas posed by money and spiritual aspiration. Money is a gift. Not "how much" money. Not "whose" money. Not "having" or "not having" money. I mean the fact of money, the nature of money, the dilemma-ridden burden of money, the sheer and subtle torment of the thing. These all function in human lives as gifts. I have argued that money is a magic most powerful, and it will draw confessions out of you about what you believe in, what you trust, what you fear most, what you will let come close. Money is an automatic teller of the soul's secrets, the soul's fears and yearnings and needs — and skills. Money makes acquaintance between strangers, between individuals or cultures, and between a person and their own soul.

Human intimacy is the hard negotiation between being open and being careful. People are often accused of hiding *from* intimacy, but more often we hide *in* intimacy. A yearning for intimacy stirs a taste for something soulful, but it is a taste that is very different for men and women. Knowing these differences will give you a chance in love and clues as to your soul's desires. It is a mistake to look for the soul in soft, comfortable places. Your soul knows better than that, and it will take you, often kicking and screaming, where it needs to go. That is your soul stirring; it only *feels* like chaos.

The torment in money is an ancient one. Why do we treat money as the root of all evil? Why does it feel dirty? The exchange of gifts, getting paid, owing a debt, borrowing and lending, envying what someone has, almsgiving, having money or not having it — all of these set up relationships between people and all of them invoke a kind of intimacy between people — a relationship of proximity, first and foremost, not a relationship of preference. One of the principal conditions of intimacy is naïveté, and for most of us a lot of naïveté gathers around money. Money is a principal agent of betrayal in intimacy, but it can also be an agent of intimacy. Money has a genius in this regard.

From the nature of human intimacy and the qualities of human soulfulness that are available to all of us there comes a story of the inevitability of suffering and loss, and we have looked at how that can happen. The suffering is most intensified in the experience of betrayal, and betrayals large or small are an inevitable thing in intimacy. Anyone who doesn't seem to share your view of how things are or should be — like a friend who tells a truth you don't want to hear or a spouse who won't go along with you — seems to betray you. Yet betrayal carries within it a way to great wisdom as well as a way to cynicism. There is a choice. While there is never a good reason to seek out betrayal, and left to our own devices we avoid it by almost any means necessary, there is no cause for alarm: betrayal is looking for each of us, to relieve us of the humiliating, infantilizing burden of naïveté. Your breaking heart makes room for your soul's work to be done.

What sower walked over earth
which hands sowed
our inward seeds of fire?
They went out from his fists like rainbow curves

to frozen earth, young loam, hot sand,
they will sleep there
greedily, and drink up our lives
and explode them into pieces
for the sake of a sunflower that you haven't seen
or a thistle head or a chrysanthemum.

Let the young rain of tears come.
Let the calm hands of grief come.
It's not all as evil as you think[2]
— ROLF JACOBSEN, "SUNFLOWER"

• • •

The miracle of interest on principal, the alchemy of the Multiplier Effect, the paper that is stronger than gold, the magic of *making* money — how could money not be a kind of religion? The intrigues of money are labyrinthine, and worthy of study and learning, and very difficult to master. But the rewards of doing so are soulful rewards. The best spiritual teaching suggests that you get dirty in this world. The circulation of money, which is crucial for the world's well-being, means that at any time each of us could be in Neruda's place, staggered by the wonder of something coming to us that we did not suspect was even there. It may never happen again, but the memory that it happened once can stay with you. You can be broken open by this gift and for the rest of your days be more capable of open arms and brother-feeling. Or you could be the other guy, on the other side of the fence, giving away quietly, anonymously, never knowing the consequences of your gift or where it has gone. Or you could be both. Life in its grandeur and open-heartedness offers up many chances to be both.

I have not said here that money is the way to happiness. I have not said that God wants you to be rich or that money is your right or even that money is good. I don't know what God wants or if any of those things are true. I have tried to be quieter than that. I have tried only to make an asset out of a necessity. Money or its scarcity is not far away from us most of our lives. You could say that life is conducted in the presence of money. If that is true, then it makes sense to me that engagement with money affords a continuing chance to ennoble one's life and the lives of others. It brings the opportunity to take the human instinct for the sacred out of the precinct of religious worship and into the world, where it also belongs. Messy mutual indebtedness, I am persuaded, is a midwife for personhood and for kinship. Money offers one way of bringing one's soul to the soul of the world, and that is very much needed.

Here's an excerpt from an article that came across my desk as I was finishing this book.

If you're rich when you retire you may not think you have to care about the world anymore. You need never be confronted with anything real ever again, until you die that is. Even if a person reaches 60 or 65, why do they assume that they will cease being the miserable, worried or discontented person they have been all their working lives the minute they retire? A person is resolutely uncreative, and has spent years resisting innovation in his or her workplace, but plans to take up painting the day after he or she leaves corporate life. Someone else dreams of doing charity work after living a completely selfish life for 60 years . . .

A modest proposal. Stop saving for your retirement immediately. Instead, spend your money on all the things you're currently denying yourself . . . Most importantly . . . understand that this next stage your life is a time when you will still have to work . . .

How is this better than self-denial today and conspicuous consumption when you're old? It will be better in the future . . . because it creates the necessity to work . . .[3]

This is pretty subversive stuff, especially when you consider that it came in an advertising supplement pitching mutual funds and other kinds of investments. The writer is trying to adjust people's expectations about how much pension money will be available later on, given demographic trends. But he is also, maybe without intention, plotting a course for going back to the world, for slipping past, altogether, the Fourth Temptation of doing only what you do best. This is pretty good advice, from the soul's point of view. The generations which are now struggling so mightily with money, maturity, and the meaning of life would do better if the older people would come back from their retirement condos, move back into their communities, and show the rest of us, however imperfectly, how it was done in their time. What we need is a living example of how to struggle, and of what it looks like to persevere and endure. It might be colder where we are, but we could pay them with honour and inclusion.

• • •

I came to thinking about money and the spiritual life the hard way, as most of us are likely to do. In the midst of paralyzing despair over the end of my marriage, I did privately what most people do. I wondered what I had done wrong. When most of us do that, we allow ourselves to consider only those failures we can bear contemplating. But there are others, out beyond what we think we can endure. Talking with a few good friends, the kind that tell you the truth when you are down, gave me my first hint that maybe there were some problems with money in there somehow, problems with the way money had been thought about and not thought about, done and not done. To be sure, we are blind in the places where we misplace our instincts. This news, that maybe money had screwed things up, a message so beneath me at the time, came as an unsuspected, shattering come-down.

At the time I had very little money, and it took a good while afterwards to make my own. I have been in both places, in having and not having. It might seem that having money gives you a kind of cushion, the luxury or comfort of contemplating these issues at a distance according to your inclinations, at your leisure. You might think that having little or no money brings the dead certainties of money hourly to your door and to your awareness, so that you are inescapably keener in your savvy about your money and your soul. My experience is that there is no inherent merit or nobility or wisdom or compassion that comes to the rich or the middling or the poor person. The presence or absence of money by itself doesn't generate any wisdom; it only brings experience. You might think it inevitable that the poor one envies the rich, but the rich one just as inevitably envies the poorer one or his own poorer days: same problems, more zeros, as they say. The envy of one, as far as I can tell, is no more defensible or noble than the envy of the other.

This meditation has been mainly about work. It has been about the work the soul must do while nailed to the wheel of the world. The direction of soul work is always this way: out of the Garden, into the world. *Spending your money is soul work*, just as saving money is. Giving money and losing money and living with or without it — all are soul work. There must be no retirement from this kind of work. This is the inheritance we really owe our children. It is just as Rumi said eight centuries ago: spend *something* — which means spend something of yourself — and be part of the exchanging flow.

Notes

Chapter 1: The Darkness in Money

1 Juan Ramon Jiminez, "I Am Not I," *Forty Poems*, ed. R. Bly (Madison, WI: Sixties Press, 1967).

2 Russel Lockhart et al., *Soul and Money* (Dallas: Spring Publications, 1982), p. 35.

3 Antonio Machado, *Times Alone: Selected Poems of Antonio Machado*, trans. and ed. R. Bly (Middletown, CT: Wesleyan University Press, 1983), p. 113.

4 Jorge Luis Borges, "The Zahir." *Labyrinths: Selected Stories and Other Writings*, ed. J.E. Irby and D.A. Yates (New York: New Directions Publishing Corp., 1981).

5 Malidoma Somé, *Of Water and the Spirit* (New York: Penguin, 1994), p. 8.

6 Sigmund Freud, "Character and Anal Eroticism" in Jackson, ed., *The Oxford Book of Money*, pp. 42–43.

Chapter 2: Usury, The Shadow of Money

1 Lewis Hyde, *The Gift: Imagination and the Erotic Life of Property* (New York: Vintage Books, 1979), pp. 111ff.

2 Ibid., p. 117.

3 Hyde, *The Gift*, p. 118.

4 Ibid., p. 120.

5 Hyde, *The Gift*, p. 125.

6 Martin Luther in Kevin Jackson, ed., *The Oxford Book of Money* (Oxford: Oxford University Press, 1995), p. 147.

7 Luther, *Deuteronomy with Annotations* (1524), qtd. in Hyde, *The Gift*, pp. 125–126.

8 Hyde, *The Gift*, p. 127.

9 Ibid., p. 132.

Chapter 3: Money and Civilization

1 Marco Polo, qtd. in Kevin Jackson, ed., *The Oxford Book of Money* (Oxford: Oxford University Press, 1995), p. 134ff.
2 Ibid., p. 135.
3 Dudley Young, *Origins of the Sacred: The Ecstasies of Love and War* (New York: St. Martin's Press, 1991), p. xxi.
4 Thomas Wiseman, *The Money Motive* (New York: Random House, 1974), p. 24.
5 Russel Lockhart et al., *Soul and Money* (Dallas: Spring Publications, 1982), p. 36.
6 W.H. Auden in Jackson, ed., *The Oxford Book of Money*, p. 42.
7 Wiseman, *The Money Motive*, p. 23.
8 Ibid., p. 18.
9 Wiseman, *The Money Motive*, p. 21.
10 Lewis Hyde, *The Gift: Imagination and the Erotic Life of Property* (New York: Vintage Books, 1979), p. 10.
11 Ibid.
12 Qtd. in Wiseman, *The Money Motive*, p. 50.
13 Qtd. in Robert Bly, ed., *The Soul Is Here for Its Own Joy*, trans. C. Barks (Hopewell, NJ: The Ecco Press, 1995), p. 64.
14 Jean de Brébeuf, *The Huron Relation of 1635* (Midland, ON: Martyr's Shrine Pub., 1972), p. 33.
15 George Eastman, *The Soul of the Indian* (Lincoln, NE: University of Nebraska Press, 1911), p. 101.
16 Jerry Mander, *In the Absence of the Sacred* (San Francisco: Sierra Club Books, 1991), p. 276.
17 Hyde, *The Gift*, p. 30.
18 American Senator Dawes, late nineteenth century, qtd. in Mander, *In the Absence of the Sacred*, p. 276.

Chapter 4: Money in Men's Lives

1 Robert Bly, *The Sibling Society* (Reading, MA: Addison Wesley,

1996), pp. viiiff.

2 Tim Lilburn, *Moosewood Sandhills* (Toronto: McClelland and Stewart, 1994), p. 30.

3 Robert Bly, "December 23, 1926," *Selected Poems* (New York: Harper and Row, 1986).

4 Jon Krakauer, *Into the Wild* (New York: Anchor Books, 1996), np.

5 Ibid., p. 115.

6 Krakauer, *Into the Wild* p. 155.

7 Ibid., p. 123.

8 Krakauer, *Into the Wild*, p. 115.

9 Ibid., p. 121.

10 Thomas Wiseman, *The Money Motive* (New York: Random House, 1974), p. 186.

11 Dostoyevsky, qtd. in Kevin Jackson, ed., *The Oxford Book of Money* (Oxford: Oxford University Press, 1995), p. 22.

12 Keats, qtd. in Ibid., p. 66.

Chapter 5: Money, Sex, Betrayal

1 James Hillman, in Russel Lockhart et al., *Soul and Money* (Dallas: Spring Publications, 1982), p. 41.

2 Thomas Wiseman, *The Money Motive* (New York: Random House, 1974), p. 223.

3 Qtd. in Kevin Jackson, ed. *The Oxford Book of Money* (Oxford: Oxford University Press, 1995), p. 32.

4 Qtd. in Ibid., p. 27.

Chapter 6: The Soul's Gold

1 William Stafford, "A Ritual to Read to Each Other" in *The Darkness around Us Is Deep: Selected Poems of William Stafford*, ed. Robert Bly (New York: HarperCollins, 1993).

2 Greg Mogenson, *God Is a Trauma: Vicarious Religion and Soul Making* (Dallas: Spring Publications, 1989), p. 14.

3 Dudley Young, *Origins of the Sacred: The Ecstasies of Love and War* (New York: St. Martin's Press, 1991), p. xxi.
4 William Wordsworth, "The World Is Too Much with Us" in Robert Bly et al., eds., *The Rag and Bone Shop of the Heart* (New York: HarperCollins, 1992), p. 476.
5 Tim Lilburn, "Contemplation Is Mourning," *Moosewood Sandhills* (Toronto: McClelland and Stewart, 1994).
6 Russel Lockhart et al., *Soul and Money* (Dallas: Spring Publications, 1982), p. 37.
7 James Hillman, qtd. in Lockhart, Ibid., p. 38.
8 Robert Bly, ed., *The Soul Is Here for Its Own Joy* (Hopewell, NJ: The Ecco Press, 1995), p. 161.

Chapter 7: Forgiveness

1 Lewis Hyde, *The Gift: Imagination and the Erotic Life of Property* (New York: Vintage Books, 1979), p. 10.
2 Qtd. in Hyde, *The Gift*, p. 11.
3 Rainer Maria Rilke, *Selected Poems of Rainer Maria Rilke*, trans. R. Bly (New York: Harper and Row, 1981), p. 13.
4 Martín Prechtel, *Long Life, Honey in the Heart* (New York: Tarcher/Putnam Books, 1999), p. 349.

Chapter 8: Conclusion: Breathing Deep the Fragrance of This World

1 Qtd. in Lewis Hyde, *The Gift: Imagination and the Erotic Life of Property* (New York: Vintage Books, 1979), p. 281.
2 In Robert Bly et al., eds., *The Rag and Bone Shop of the Heart* (New York: HarperCollins, 1992), p. 111.
3 Kevin Browne, *Saturday Night* (February 1998), p. 92.

Bibliography

Bly, Robert. *Meditations on the Insatiable Soul.* New York: HarperCollins, 1994.

——. *Selected Poems.* New York: Harper and Row, 1986.

——. *The Sibling Society.* Reading, MA: Addison-Wesley, 1996.

——. ed. *The Soul Is Here for Its Own Joy.* Hopewell, NJ: The Ecco Press, 1995.

Bly, Robert, et al. *The Rag and Bone Shop of the Heart.* New York: HarperCollins, 1992.

Borges, Jorge Luis. *Labyrinths: Selected Stories and Other Writings.* Eds. J.E. Irby and D.A. Yates. New York, NY: New Directions Publishing Corp., 1981.

de Brébeuf, Jean. *The Huron Relation of 1635.* Midland, ON: Martyr's Shrine Pub., 1972.

Catlin, George. *North American Indians.* Ed. Peter Matthiessen. 1841; New York: Penguin Books, 1989.

Eastman, George. *The Soul of the Indian.* Lincoln, NE: University of Nebraska Press, 1911.

Ellul, Jacques. *Money and Power.* Downers Grove, IL: Intervarsity Press, 1985.

Haan, Roelf. *The Economics of Honour: Biblical Reflections on Money and Property.* Geneva: WCC Publications, 1988.

Hillman, James. *Loose Ends.* Dallas: Spring Publications, 1975.

——. *The Soul's Code.* New York: Random House, 1996.

Hillman, James, and Michael Ventura. *We've Had a Hundred Years of Psychotherapy and the World's Getting Worse.* San Francisco, HarperCollins, 1992.

Hyde, Lewis. *The Gift: Imagination and the Erotic Life of Property.* New York: Vintage Books, 1979.

Jackson, Kevin, ed. *The Oxford Book of Money*. Oxford: Oxford University Press, 1995.

Jiminez, Juan Ramon. *Forty Poems*. Ed. R. Bly. Madison, WI: Sixties Press, 1967.

———. *God Desired and Desiring*. Trans. A. de Nicolas. New York: Paragon House, 1987.

Kane, Sean. *Wisdom of the Myth Tellers*. Peterborough, ON: Broadview Press, 1994.

Krakauer, Jon. *Into the Wild*. New York: Anchor Books, 1996.

Lilburn, Tim. *Moosewood Sandhills*. Toronto: McClelland and Stewart, 1994.

Lockhart, Russel, et al. *Soul and Money*. Dallas: Spring Publications, 1982.

Machado, Antonio. *Times Alone: Selected Poems of Antonio Machado*. Trans. and Ed. R. Bly. Middletown, CT: Wesleyan University Press, 1983.

Mander, Jerry. *In the Absence of the Sacred*. San Francisco: Sierra Club Books, 1991.

Meade, Michael. *Men and the Water of Life*. San Francisco: HarperCollins, 1993.

Mogenson, Greg. *God Is a Trauma: Vicarious Religion and Soul Making*. Dallas: Spring Publications, 1989.

"Money," *Granta*, no. 49 (Fall 1994).

Needleman, Jacob. *Money and the Meaning of Life*. New York: Doubleday, 1991.

Nowlan, Alden. *What Happened When He Went to the Store for Bread*. Ed. Thomas R. Smith. St. Paul, MN: Nineties Press, 1993.

O'Kane, Françoise. *Sacred Chaos: Reflections on God's Shadow and the Dark Self*. Toronto: Inner City Books, 1990.

Prechtel, Martín. *Long Life, Honey in the Heart*. New York: Tarcher/Putnam Books, 1999.

Ramsay, Jay. *Alchemy: The Art of Transformation.* San Francisco: HarperCollins, 1997.

Rilke, Rainer Maria. *Selected Poems of Rainer Maria Rilke.* Trans. R. Bly. New York: Harper and Row, 1981.

Rumi. *Delicious Laughter.* Trans. C. Barks. Atlanta: Maypop Books, 1990.

Somé, Malidoma. *Of Water and the Spirit.* New York: Penguin, 1994.

Stackhouse, Max, et al., eds. *On Moral Business: Classical and Contemporary Resources for Ethics in Economic Life.* Grand Rapids, MI: Eerdmans, 1995.

Stafford, William. *The Darkness around Us Is Deep: Selected Poems of William Stafford.* Ed. R. Bly. New York: Harper-Collins, 1993.

von Franz, Marie-Louise. *Projection and Re-Collection in Jungian Psychology: Reflections of the Soul.* London: Open Court, 1980.

———. *Shadow and Evil in Fairy Tales.* Boston, MA: Shambhala Pub., 1995.

Wiseman, Thomas. *The Money Motive.* New York: Random House, 1974.

Young, Dudley. *Origins of the Sacred: The Ecstasies of Love and War.* New York: St. Martin's Press, 1991.

Zornberg, Avivah. *The Beginning of Desire: Reflections on Genesis.* New York: Doubleday, 1995.

Permissions

Excerpt from "A Ritual to Read to Each Other" copyright ©
1960, 1998 by the estate of William Stafford. Reprinted from
The Way It Is: New & Selected Poems with the permission of
Graywolf Press, Saint Paul, Minnesota.

Excerpts from *Into the Wild* by Jon Krakauer, copyright © 1996
by Jon Krakauer. Used by permission of Villard Books, a
division of Random House, Inc.

Excerpts from *The Gift* by W. Lewis Hyde, copyright © 1979,
1980, 1983 by W. Lewis Hyde. Used by permission of Random
House, Inc.

Moosewood Sandhills by Tim Lilburn. Used by permission,
McClelland & Stewart Ltd., *The Canadian Publishers.*